note to self

also by connor franta

A Work in Progress

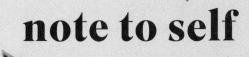

note to self

connor franta

Keywords

PRESS

ATRIA

New York   London   Toronto   Sydney   New Delhi

ATRIA
BOOKS

Imprints of Simon & Schuster, Inc.
1230 Avenue of the Americas
New York, NY 10020

First Keywords Press / Atria Books edition April 2017

Keywords Press /**ATRIA** BOOKS and colophons are trademarks of Simon & Schuster, Inc.

For information about special discounts for bulk purchases, please contact Simon & Schuster Special Sales at 1-866-506-1949 or business@simonandschuster.com.

The Simon & Schuster Speakers Bureau can bring authors to your live event. For more information or to book an event, contact the Simon & Schuster Speakers Bureau at 1-866-248-3049 or visit our website at www.simonspeakers.com.

Manufactured in the United States of America

10 9 8 7 6 5 4 3 2

Library of Congress Cataloging-in-Publication Data
Names: Franta, Connor.
Title: Note to self / Connor Franta.
Description: First Keywords Press hardcover edition. | New York : Keywords Press, 2017.
Identifiers: LCCN 2016054990 (print) | LCCN 2017008802 (ebook) | ISBN 9781501158018 (hardcover) | ISBN 9781501158094 (ebook)
Subjects: LCSH: Franta, Connor, 1992– | Internet personalities—United States—Biography. | Entrepreneurs—United States—Biography. | YouTube (Electronic resource)
Classification: LCC PN2287.F6735 A3 2017 (print) | LCC PN2287.F6735 (ebook) | DDC 792.028092 [B] —dc23
LC record available at https://lccn.loc.gov/2016054990

ISBN 978-1-5011-5801-8
ISBN 978-1-5011-5809-4 (ebook)

for me

contents

contents

contents

They say the truth will set you free, but what they neglect to mention is what happens when the truth isn't what you want to hear.

introduction

I'm a private person, ironically. "Ironic" because I'm in the business of public disclosure, and I'm part of a generation that shares everything. Aside from my daily social posts that allow glimpses into my life, I tend to keep my thoughts, opinions, and words to myself—relatively speaking. Now, if you get me around the few people I trust, I'll say just about anything that comes to mind. *Anything.* So don't try me. I'll let my mind spill its contents like a cup with no lid, whether those contents are applicable to the moment or not. I'll dish it all.

On the flip side, where the general public is concerned, I often remain silent. I like to think of myself as a listener—an observer. I enjoy absorbing information and analyzing my surroundings, even down to the color

1

of the shoes the girl across the room is wearing (mustard). It's more by choice than habit. I derive a strange thrill from noticing the details of my surroundings, and I always have.

But there's also a dark underpinning to my silence. Sometimes, I can't decide if what I'm thinking is what others want to know. Do people really care that some strange girl across the room is wearing mustard-colored shoes? I'm putting my money on the answer being *no*. If I voice my thoughts, will it disturb the atmosphere? Upset the dynamics of the present moment? Is my input even worth sharing?

I think I think too much (as will become clear in the pages ahead), but that's who I am, and that's what I'm here to share: my perspective, intimate musings, odd observations, intense moments, and the interior dialogue I reserve for only myself and a select few. This book is filled with short essays. Observations. Poems. Thoughts. Feelings. Ups. Downs. And the in-betweens. I'd like to think of this book as a scrapbook of my mind. A collection of small vulnerabilities. A harmony of notes to self.

Growing up and discovering independence brings with it the realization that this world is not all cotton candy and giggles. When we let go of our security blankets—parents, siblings, childhood home, and familiar surroundings—and stand on our own two feet—being accountable, minimizing negative consequences, and navigating life's everyday challenges on our own—the more we see society's true colors, and the more we become aware of what really goes on behind seemingly perfect but staged scenes: the social masks we all wear, the brave fronts we put up, and the curated personas that don't align with who we truly are.

I'm saying this from a place of dramatic privilege, and I don't mean to come across like I have it hard, or have all the answers. But I'm speaking from a plethora of experiences that, while particular to me, might be relevant to you as well. I've managed to fake it this far and, somehow, I've been able to make it work.

I'm a twenty-four-year-old man, and in my six years of adulthood, I've experienced some of the highest highs this world has to offer. I've traveled to more than a dozen countries in the past two years, become the CEO of three individual companies, made an incredible living, met some of the most amazing people I believe this world has to offer, and accidentally fallen head over heels in love along the way. Each experience, and accompanying learning curve, has shaped me into the person I am today, opening my eyes and altering my point of view in ways I never thought possible. But not every day is a good day.

During my journey as a young gay man who deals with mild depression, anxiety, and frequent self-inflicted mental abuse—worries, insecurities, defeatist thinking—I've been in the dirt and trudged through the lowest of low periods. I've been depressed to the point of entertaining irrational thoughts to end it all. I've been used and mistreated for personal gain. I've been broken up with, and left broken. I've gone through what I know to be my darkest moments. But I'm not here to throw a pity party or complain; I'm only here to share. Because it's through the universal experiences of life that we can all connect and relate to each other. For me, the only way to climb out of the pits I sometimes find myself in is through the guidance and assistance of others. Our words, our firsthand experiences, our shared truths can form ladders. And bring hope to others.

Yes, on the surface, I've had an exceptional life so far, and I couldn't be more grateful for every second. But if you allow me to dive deeper, you'll see that I, like everyone else, struggle. I'm imperfect. Flawed. Damaged and broken at times. But human. And I try to embrace this existence for what it is: a beautiful mess.

Without the "worst," the "best" wouldn't taste as sweet. No sailor, no fisherman, no captain of a ship has ever earned his stripes on calm waters. Storms, internal and external, enable me to develop my character and become stronger. Of course, it's easy to assume that money, fame, and luxury can win over sadness, but that's far from the truth. I really wish it were true. I do. I wish those benefits took away the stress of others constantly watching, talking, assuming, examining, judging, scrutinizing, bashing, and shaming—which is something that everyone deals with, whether they're in the public eye or not. I wish I didn't let the words of others stick with me for so long. I wish my thoughts weren't self-defeating at times. But when I leap into wormholes of utter negativity, it's difficult to find my way back out . . . and status, success, and good fortune *don't* provide a ladder out of the pit.

If my first book, *A Work in Progress*, was a reflection of my external life so far, then this follow-up is a reflection of my interior life right now, and all the things that concern me—not so much a continuation of my story but more of a deepening. I'm here to spew my madness on the page and, perhaps, make a little sense of it along the way. Writing is my therapy. Sorting it out has, in the end, proven cathartic.

Much of what you're about to read was written in the heat of the moment. The darkest passages came to me with tears in my eyes and darkness clouding my mind. The happiest of times were recorded moments after they happened, if only to preserve them in text. My words were placed on paper—or tapped into my phone—when certain thoughts, emotions, and inspirations hit home. I've tried to maintain that rawness and sense of authenticity throughout. If you read a piece on its own, you might say it doesn't make sense or seems random, but when taken all together, these pieces form my grasp on reality.

I'm just trying to be honest and shed light on what's real to me. This is life: confusing, difficult, stressful, filled with heightened emotions and irrational actions and decisions. We don't always mean what we say, and we don't always say what we believe, but I wanted to capture these moments nevertheless, without the polish of hindsight.

What you're about to read is the closest thing to my heart and soul that I have ever produced for anyone else to read. I'm cracking the door open a little wider. It's not as self-edited as *A Work in Progress* was; after all, that was my first memoir—the way I wanted to be seen. No. This is an open diary. This gives my insides a voice through visuals and poetry; this is me spilled out on paper.

Each and every one of us experiences the human condition. That is our great equalizer, our common ground, our reason for empathy. We live in a curative space of perfection, especially in today's world. I'm not happy a lot of the time, and I feel shame about that. It's been hard for me to find another open soul to confide in and relate my story to. Until now, perhaps. This one is for you. But, more importantly, this one is for me.

Spring 2016

welcome to my happy place

It's 7:43 p.m. A brisk breeze sweeps over one of the highest peaks in view, into the valley below, and back to where it originated in the clouded sky. I'm nothing but calm right now. The cool air smells and feels so pure. It's that nice kind of cold that isn't too cold, creating a post-sunset chill that feels just right. Goose bumps cover my arms and legs, but I don't care that my shorts and T-shirt now seem ill-considered. I don't care because, honestly, how could I? How could I think of anything else beyond the beauty that lies in front of me?

This is one of those places I've longed to visit but, for some reason, have never made the extra effort to see, even though it's just a fifteen-minute drive outside of San Francisco. But today, today I made the trip. I promised myself when I woke up this morning that I'd be here when the sun went down, and I'm holding myself accountable to that intention, to park my butt on this grassy hill overlooking the Golden Gate Bridge and the famous bay it spans.

The moment I stepped out of the car after being dropped off, I smiled more than I have in months, and I'm not exaggerating. Finally, after all these years, I was seeing this amazing landmark paired with a setting sun so vibrant—almost loud, in a way—that it would put all others to shame. I couldn't help but giggle, like a giddy kid on Christmas morning, filled from my feet to my ears with utter joy. This might sound super-silly and slightly overstated to the average person, but not to me. No, no. Because for the longest time, I had imagined what it would be like for me to be here, in this very spot, in this happy place—a hunch that turns out to be right.

I'm unplugged. Disconnected from everything but this moment. Not a single distraction. Not a single care. It's just me and this view. There's nowhere else in the entire world I want to be as I, along with groups of tourists, climb the hill to see the bridge in its full, golden glory.

I gasp, genuinely overcome with awe at the magnificent sight. The bridge is MASSIVE. I can't believe humans made this. The light from the setting sun drenches the sky in color, forming a warm backdrop for the bridge. Streaks of red, orange, pink, and blue. I remind myself that this beautiful scene is changing every minute, and I need to take in every stage—be present for every single moment. I become consumed with capturing nature's work of art in different ways. I'm talking DSLR, iPhone, Boomerangs, time-lapse videos, panoramas, THE WORKS. Nothing will compare to the reality I'm experiencing, but that's all right—I want to really live in, and relive, this moment over and over.

I'm trying my best not to succumb to my tech impulses, but I can't help myself. My passions come alive when I see something this beautiful, and I'm weirdly driven to try to translate what I see to the screen. This scene will never be seen again as my eyes see it now, but I can do my best. So that's what I do. I'm running all over this hill, standing on poles, peeking through fences, lying on the ground among flowers; you name it, I'm trying all angles. Even though I might look like an idiot, I honestly don't care. I don't know the people around me. Nothing matters in this moment other than the moment itself. I'm happy to enjoy its company.

Before I know it, I come back to reality. When I look down at my phone, an hour has somehow flown by. Eight forty-five p.m.? *Whoa.* I totally zoned out. That's never really happened to me before, at least to this extent. But I guess when I lost myself in the moment, time lost itself to my joy. And, to me, these moments are what life is all about.

The light is fading fast; it's gotten significantly colder, and the people who were around me have drifted away, disappearing quicker than the sun that now hides behind the hilltops. In front of me, the city of San Francisco is still alive with light—a glittering landscape, with cars zooming around, buildings illuminated, and the largest, clearest moon I've ever laid eyes on rising like a balloon. As soon as I think this night can't get any better, it does. No exaggeration, it's hypnotic.

My body begins to quiver. Not from excitement (I'm not that much of a nerd! . . . Well, I am, but whatever) but because it's now freezing. I throw on the sweater I was given earlier in the day by Twitter (<3 u), and continue my mad attempt to capture the scene; to honor it; to frame the memory; to remember how it feels to be in this spot. I feel almost spiritual just by being here, which, from someone who's not too spiritual, is saying something.

This will emerge as one of the more memorable moments of my life so far, and I'm really not sure why. Maybe it's because I had eagerly anticipated what my happy place would feel like, and it exceeded all expectations. Maybe it was a simple, soulful moment that required no internal editing or filtering, no explanation. Or maybe it was a moment of pure joy that, deep down, I needed to feel alive again after going through some of the hardest months of my adult life. I'm not sure. But what I do know is that the time I spent on that hilltop— roughly two hours—flew by and left me wanting more. More time alone. More of these magical moments. More time to reflect. More time to appreciate the natural good in the world.

I went up there alone, empty-handed. I left alone, but walked away with a unique memory no one else will have; it was mine and mine alone to treasure. That's so special to me. As I grow older, I wish for more of these snapshots of joy, to be able to string them together into a long line of happiness. To remember how life should feel. To remember to take time out by myself and appreciate both my own company and the world around me. The world is filled with happy places, but sometimes I forget to look for them or fail to see that I'm already in a happy place.

It's impossible to recreate an experience exactly, especially one of such significance. No single experience can ever be the same or bring out the same emotional response. I could return to that same spot at sunset a month, a year, or a decade from now, and it would be different. But after that night, I'll be looking a bit harder to stay present, paying better attention to individual moments of fleeting magic. It's about making more of these memories, not about trying to remake them. That's what this night was all about: it left me craving that feeling again—to be in my happy place and watch the world slow down to a near-stop while I sit, watch, wait, and listen.

I had dreamt about this solo mission for years, as cheesy as that sounds. Yet I never imagined it would leave such a lasting impression. I went there to live out a dream, and I left enriched with a memory. That's something I couldn't have planned or predicted. Ultimately, the value of an experience is largely left to chance, and I was lucky that this particular one wasn't a letdown. At all.

In a way, I'm leaving a lot of my life up to chance these days. I'm leading a march of self-discovery into a thick forest, with no compass to guide me. Moments of glory, such as the one just described, let me know that I'm heading in the right direction. What direction that is, I don't precisely know. I still feel so fucking lost, but that's all right. That's just how it is now. I'll keep moving forward because standing still is not an option. You don't find your happy places in life without putting one foot in front of the other.

lemons cakes in a better place

light like a lemon cake
tickles like a feather
at the corners of my lips
makes them rise
for this moment
smells of sweet caramel
jolt my brain
back to life
the past matters less
for i am greater
than before
i was
so little
now bigger i stand
on my two feet
held by my own
taller than ever

unspoken bonds

I'm sure I'm not the only one who has convinced himself that no one else has ever gone through, or is going through, the same angst/turmoil/upsetting experience. *No one understands my sadness. Not one person gets how it feels to be this jealous. Who has ever been as confused as I am right now? How could anyone ever understand me?!*

These are the kinds of thoughts that come into play every time I experience an intense feeling. I immediately isolate myself, thinking no one will understand, so why bother trying to explain? But you know what's crazy? Emotions are *the* single most relatable thing out there. They represent a kind of unspoken bond that we share but, for some reason, are often reluctant to acknowledge.

And yet when I'm going through a tough time, I feel so alone, led by the mistaken belief that my sweltering feelings are somehow unique to me.

Everyone knows what it's like to be happy, sad, angry, or frustrated, and most of us can probably pinpoint a time when we felt those emotions the strongest. Sure, we experience them at different levels of intensity; my worst day will be completely different from yours. But we *can* identify with what someone is going through. And we can empathize with one another—that's how we relate to each other. That's our point of connection. That's how a sixteen-year-old can talk to a sixty-five-year-old and find common ground. Because life is a *feeling* experience. All of us, no matter who we are or where we come from, feel something on some level. Acknowledge and accept that fact, and it becomes comforting. It means none of us is alone.

My struggle, my pain, my grief, my despair, my tears—they're not uncommon. They're shared. And once something is shared, it loses its isolating potential. That's something I've come to realize—once I understood that I'm experiencing something that millions of others have endured before, and are enduring at the same time, it somehow makes it feel less frightening, less heavy, less individual.

Nowadays, when life starts to feel like a little too much, and when a certain emotion overwhelms me, I remind myself that I'm not the only person to ever feel this way. That makes it less daunting to speak up and reach out to a close friend or family member who can be by my side. No one is alone, however scary a feeling might be. And good people will be there for one another. The only difference behind one feeling or the next is the story behind it, but explaining that story lightens the load and, I guarantee you, does wonders in helping to ease the pain.

to my dearest past

Picture this: young Connor at the awkward age of
twelve, on the verge of receiving his first spark of
real-world awareness in the form of insecurity, ambition,
and independence, all mixed together in a prepubescent
stew of hormones and budding sexuality. Gross. Mother
Nature has a twisted sense of humor, but twelve was
also the age when everything began to change for me
(literally). A year later, I would realize I was gay and
begin to transform into a young man (further discovering
that puberty is one bitch of a process), and then, during
my later teen years, my eyes would finally open up to the
colorful and deeply complex world around me. At that
point, I stopped merely existing and began considering
who I was and what I wanted to be as a person. Once

the innocence was wiped clean from my eyes, I saw life for what it is: complicated.

What follows is an open letter to all of those versions of my past self, from the age of twelve and onward. If I'd actually received this note in real life, maybe it would've made things a whole lot easier . . .

Hi Connor. Sorry if this is all over the place but, as you know, my mind is pure chaos, always going off in a million directions at once. You understand.

It's nice to be in a position where I can look back and reassure you that things are good for you now. I generally radiate a certain glow of happiness. I know you understand that this wasn't always the case. In fact, I hesitate to even invoke your understanding because we both know how consistently fragile we are. But when I step outside of myself, I see so much growth. I see years of change leading up to this current version of me. I can connect the dots and see where they've led me. But please take note, Past Me: this transformation took YEARS. And often times, it went completely unnoticed, even by me; it's only in hindsight that I see that long path I've walked to reach this leg of the race. I now see and understand you, Past Me, more clearly than you see yourself. In fact, I understand young Connor better than I understand current Connor. Your life has been a silent struggle; a roller coaster in the dark, sending you in directions that you least expect, and jerking you from side to side. And then, just as you see light at the end of the tunnel, you spiral back down into the abyss and keep on twirling and twisting in endless circles.

You won't immediately realize it, but this tumultuous decade

*of growth that lies ahead of you—from twelve to twenty-two—is
something you'll be grateful for one day. Crazy, I know. But you
will cherish the torture you put yourself through. You'll live the
highest of highs and the lowest of lows. You'll know a level of fame
and fortune that you only understand from the movies you see on
Friday nights with your friends and family in your tiny, rural oasis.
Along with that, you'll experience intense self-loathing behind
closed doors, bringing you within inches of doing something you
know you'd regret. But these struggles don't need to be validated in
text. You know how far south things have gone, and only you can
feel the feelings you feel. Only you can fully understand what those
experiences did to you. No one else.*

*But you know what, buddy? I have a surprise for you: through
it all, you'll resurface stronger and wiser than ever before. I'm
happy to say you're still here, still kicking, still soaring into the year
2017. You're thriving! Look at you! I'm writing to you from a point
in time when you'll be able to take a breath, look out over the
horizon, and be thankful. You'll get here, but it won't be without a
lot of effort, I might add.*

*Here's the deal: the train tracks are taking you places that you
didn't think you'd go, so try to sit back and let the ride commence.
Don't fight it; enjoy it. On the way, you'll entertain doubts and
wonder what the hell you're doing. Rest assured, these years—this
inexplicable journey—will shape your future and, more importantly,
your character, for the better and the best. Trust in yourself because,
more often than not, you'll be the only one who believes in your
vision. Others will see what you do, but they might not see it so read-
ily. They just need time. Don't let them slow you down. Don't let*

ANYONE slow you down. Stay on track. Stay true to your vision.

Because you were emotionally at war with yourself from a young age, you'll have to learn how to see the world, not just look at it. This will be your greatest tool, and the only way you'll be able to find your place in the world. You're a soulful guy, and you have to trust your instinct to lead you forward the same way Waze navigates drivers around Los Angeles. Resist the urge to take a more traditional route; your path to happiness is a far different one that sometimes seems like it'll be quicker but ends up just being an anxiety-ridden pain in the ass. But it'll be worth it.

I see you now, in high school: a chameleon, molding your-self to fit whatever social circle you're with at the moment: male, female, athletic, intellectual, political; heck, even religious. People say our teenage years are the most difficult years, and that's most definitely true. For a lot of kids, that has to do with feeling like an outsider. Your problem is a little different. You're so wonderfully naive, like a human version of Bambi (if you add green eyes and a mop of sandy blond hair), and people embrace you for your inno-cence and good nature. When you get to high school, you'll have great friends, take AP classes, and help lead your cross-country team to state championships. But, to a certain extent, your trail was blazed for you by your sister and your brother. You're being grand-fathered into a nice life—at least on paper. None of this privilege will diminish your internal struggles. Beneath the surface, you're a bomb ready to explode. And what's sad is that you want to explode. You almost wish for it to just . . . happen already.

Insecurity infests your mind like a swarm of bees, buzzing too loudly for you to think straight (literally). From your small size,

*to your struggle with weight, to your constantly cracking voice,
to your secrets about your sexuality . . . the sadness is heavy. I get
it. And you've learned to hide it so damn well that no one has a
fucking clue. You're a good secret keeper—so good that Mom and
Dad don't have a single clue that you hate yourself, that you resent
everything about who you are, and that a river of anger runs deep
in your veins. Please. Please just listen and understand that they
don't check in with you and ask if you're all right because, to
them, you appear to be a near-perfect angel. They don't know any
better. They can't hear what you scream in your mind 24/7. They
can't hear you yell "I HATE MYSELF" every night when the
bedroom door closes and you remove that mask you wear, day in
and day out.*

*And here's the thing: they won't hear any of it for a good ten
years. Which is why I'm here to remind you that I hear you, and
that you will deal with it. I know how the self-hate reverberates off
the walls of your cranium so frequently that it feels almost normalized within your already-cluttered head. You've accepted that "This
is just how it is for you." You've convinced yourself that "different"
equals "broken;" that you are broken. Unfixable. A misfit toy that
must be repaired or, better yet, trashed. To the naked eye you look
fine, but under the microscope you are flawed. But I'll let you in
on a little secret: no one else is looking through that microscope
but you. Not a single other person is fixating on the things you
magnify in your own mind. It's all in your head, so ease up on
yourself and slow down with all the worrying.*

*You silently scream "WHY CAN'T I JUST BE LIKE EVERY-
ONE ELSE?" without realizing that you already are; everyone else*

is doing what you're doing but in different ways, with different hang-ups, and with a different microscope. Everyone thinks their monsters are visible to the world, but they're not—they're figments of our overblown imaginations, warped projections of our own self-image. Once you stop seeing them, they'll fully disappear. Yes, it's that easy. I know where you are. I also know how to stop being where you are. I wish I could reach out and tell someone to hear you sooner, just to relieve some of the pain. I wish you could know that everything is going to turn out just fine; not perfect, but okay. All these worries and anxieties are merely growing pains. You'll carry the scars for a long time, unable to forget what it felt like to be you, at the age you are now. It hurts to think so poorly of yourself, doesn't it? You start to believe yourself, allowing the sadness to eat away at you from the inside until you're a hollowed-out shell. I wish I could take those thoughts away from you, but I think the mind needs to know its weaknesses before it can appreciate its strengths.

Please know that being "different" is okay. Your unique qualities—which you don't appreciate yet—will be your source of greatness in the future. They make you who you are for the better, not the worst. Please trust me when I say that you're built in a special way, but that doesn't make you broken, worthless, or expendable. It makes you, you. And that's wonderful. Believe in yourself. What a cliché, but it's a phrase that packs a sucker punch of sincerity. There will always be someone better, but that's not for you to focus on. You're not the smartest—that's for her. You're not that fastest— that's for him. You're not the most successful—that's for them. But you know what? You're the greatest that you can be—and that's

32

for you. Everyone possesses a unique set of skills and contributes different kinds of qualities to this planet, including you. No one is your particular blend of smart, kind, thoughtful, expressive, creative, empathetic, and driven. You'll see that one day. You're a bud covered in snow in the garden of your mind. Just wait for spring.

In the meantime, don't take it out on others. Your internal battles generate so much self-hatred that it occasionally leaks into the lives of loved ones. They don't deserve that. They're not doing anything wrong (most of the time). So perk up your ears when I say this: try your best to keep your anger to yourself, or at least let it out in a constructive way. You've got so much pride that when you hurt a loved one with your words and empty anger, you can't muster up a meaningful apology. Work on that. Work HARD on that. The you of the future is kind, compassionate, and level-headed; don't leave a trail of fallen trees in your wake. Relationships are hard to come by, so maintain the ones you have with care and consideration. Love your loved ones. They're easily the best part of living.

Finally, consider this wild idea: do what you want to do. Insane concept, I know. You'll waste so many years wishing and wanting to act in a play, or to take a painting class, or to sing at the top of your lungs in front of strangers, or to go to a school dance and actually dance like no one's watching. My best advice? Just fucking do it. What's the worst that could happen? Someone will laugh? At WHAT? You enjoying yourself? That's messed up on THEIR part. Not yours. Don't hold back on what makes you happy just because you fear it will make someone else uncomfortable. The more you tell yourself "no," the more normalized it becomes and the more you become separated from the real you. You lost yourself for so many years by trying to become a person you never wanted to be: the jock, the college student, the stereotypical masculine male. None of those were you, so quit playing a fool. Leave the scene for another. Trust me, you won't miss your old role for even a second. Literally.

Okay, Past Me, I'm going to leave you with one more thing before we dig deeper into this book (and it's book number two! Yes, you have that unexpected joy to look forward to): You'll be happy one day. You'll be the you that your instincts always knew you could be. Take comfort in knowing that it will happen and better yet, you will make it happen. Take the pressure off yourself a little. Relax and just . . . be.

Slowly, you'll make your way to me and you'll feel great. It's so amazing that you won't even believe it if I tried to describe it. But this is your destination. Try your best to get here in one piece. You're going to love it.

sometimes the quiet ones

are yelling on the inside

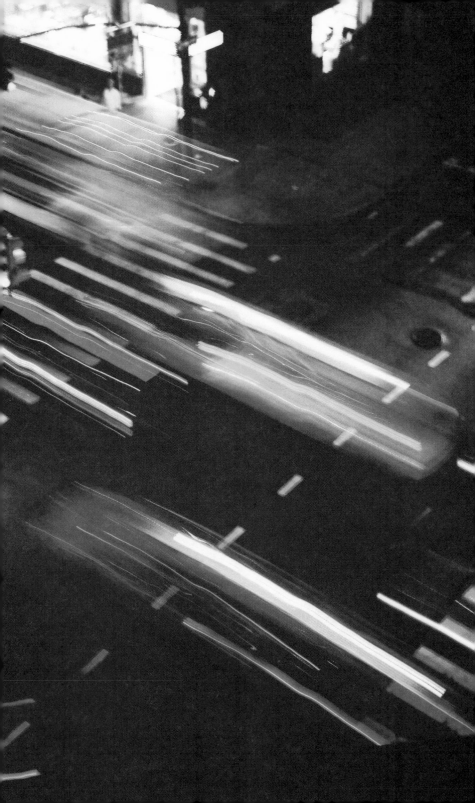

patterns

i feel good
i feel bad
i'm up
i'm down
i'm happy
i'm sad

where is the gray area
when can i be in between
oh no here we go again

i feel good
i feel bad
i'm up
i'm down
i'm happy
i'm sad

confront your greatest fears
voice your biggest problems
acknowledge your tiniest issues
the longer you stay silent
the louder they become
they won't disappear if you ignore them
they will spread and affect all aspects of your life

the thin line between fearlessness and fear

Here's something strange about me: Roller coasters, heights, bungee jumping, skydiving, flying, and rock climbing don't scare me. I don't fear planes crashing, car wrecks, or any "daredevil pursuit," really. I'm barely even fazed by things that most people seem to fear—and it kind of freaks me out that these things *don't* freak me out.

My friends continue to be surprised that I'm the type of guy who wants to sit in the front car of a roller coaster, or be the first to leap off a bridge with nothing tethering me but a bungee cord around my twenty-eight-inch waist. In those moments, my heart races to new levels of fast. I feel alive, awakened by the thrill.

I must have a disconnected wire in my central nervous system—one tha would transmit ordinary fear or panic to the brain. It's there, I'm sure, but maybe it got severed after the third bungee jump?

"Fearless Connor" seems to contradict my otherwise reserved and poised manner, and this side of me doesn't quite match my other interests or general character. But there's something about danger that excites me. I'm thrilled by doing thrilling things, by throwing myself into unusual situations that elicit a set of emotions I'm otherwise unable to experience. Now, I'm not trying to say I'm some kind of "thrill-seeker" or adrenaline junkie with a death wish; it's more that I'm unfazed whenever life takes me to the edge. I seem to have this innate trust that everything will turn out all right. Every time I find myself returning to the ledge once again, jumping becomes a little easier. I fall, leaving it to fate. That feeling—the feeling of utter trust—is what keeps me coming back for more. That process—that trust—has influenced how I view the world: with almost a blind faith.

When I went skydiving for the first time, I never once thought, *Turn this plane around and take me back to Mother Earth, GODDAMMIT!!* It was more like, *Okay . . . OKAY. Are we ready? Can I go yet? There's food down there and I'm starving.* When I'm on a plane going through heavy turbulence, I don't really bat an eye. *Well, there's nothing I can do now if this thing decides to go down, so why freak out?* *continues listening to music as the Boeing 737 hits "Ladies and gentlemen, please return to your seats and buckle the fuck up!" mode*

When I first realized this about myself, it got me thinking, *What really DOES scare me? What actually sends a shiver down my spine and keeps me up at night?*

Well, I'm downright terrified of receiving a call that something bad has happened to a close friend or family member, or discovering that one of them is suffering in some way, shape, or form that renders me helpless. I'm also rattled by the prospect of being alone for too long (not for hours, like a dog, but days or weeks, like a shut-in); not doing everything in my immediate power to achieve my goals; the idea that I'm not the person I think I am; spiders of any size (typical but worth including); and the thought of being stranded alone in the middle of the ocean with nothing and no one in sight, very much like in that movie *Cast Away*, with Tom Hanks and his BFF volleyball.

You see the pattern emerging here? I'm not terrified by reality/going to the edge/taking risks/doing things that might involve an insurance policy. But I *am* terrified by far-fetched outcomes that my mind invents: the non-reality/imagined outcomes/things that are highly unlikely to happen. Jump out of a plane? No problem. But when I merely contemplate the irrational thought of something horrible happening to a loved one? It's enough to turn me into a wreck.

A few years ago, I was driving to work at a neighboring city pool—a solid fifteen-minute trip that I had done many times. I knew the route so well that I could have driven there with my eyes shut. (Now, before you jump to any conclusions and make any stinging judgments, NO, I did not fall asleep at the wheel. It was 11 a.m. *Who* in their right mind would ever do that?) But, I sort of, um, daydreamed myself into a stupor and drifted into oncoming traffic, nearly causing a head-on collision. I was an idiot. A total daydreaming moron. What a reckless state of mind to be in while operating a motor vehicle!

But what makes this admission worse is that I derived a strange, positive feeling from this near-miss. It's hard to describe, but within seconds, and after realizing everything was fine, I felt ALIVE. Like Fate had flicked me on the earlobe and said, "Hey, you're still alive. Do what you will with that information. You're welcome, honey!" I felt good after doing something reckless. Pretty twisted, right?

I've molded this type of "fear" into a constructive emotion that, in my opinion, assists my character development, as if I need these scrapes and adrenaline rushes to remind me that I'm living, breathing, and have a pulse. WOW, what a life—and I need to appreciate that. Anything can happen at any moment, in an instant, for better or worse, and I can choose to either consciously live in fear of the unknown or melt into life's warm embrace. Me, I'm a puddle for Fate's spontaneous kiss.

Now, let's take it on the flip side.

While venturing into the industry of words (honestly, why my publisher let me become an author is BEYOND me), I've met a lot of amazing new people along the way that I otherwise wouldn't have had the pleasure of knowing. Among those people are my editors on my two books, Jhanteigh and Steve. I've come to love these two. It's gone above and beyond working together. Despite the three of us being scattered along the age spectrum, I've managed to form really strong friendships with them both. They're intelligent, kind, and thoughtful, and their editorial advice helps me sound like less of a buffoon on the page than I might have sounded had I attempted to self-publish my work. So, honestly, kudos to them. Not only I, but the world, thanks you.

But while writing this second book, I've had my heart sink twice by personal phone calls from these two. In the space of three months, they both called to share some personal news that rocked my world when I heard it. I wanted to grab hold of reality, but all I could do was fall. And that fucking sucks. Because all I felt was helplessness. There was nothing I could do or say. All I could do was be there and offer support . . . and I hated that. That's what scares me. That's *why* it scares me—I feel a sense of powerlessness when faced with bad news from people I care about. These are the types of calls that keep me up at night and make the clocks tick a little bit slower.

When it boils down to it, fear is about perspective. Fear is in the eye of the beholder, and not everyone sees it the same way. You can either live life curled up in a ball, fearful of what's around the corner, or you can turn that corner with your head held high. There are things that I'll always be afraid of, and that's how life works. But I can always overcome them. I know that I am able to conquer most of my fears along the way. So much of our story as human beings is up for interpretation. So much of what goes on can be looked at from multiple perspectives. And so I'm determined to live by one motto: don't fear being afraid.

a mindful mind

I'm sitting in the corner of a café on Melrose Avenue, nursing my overpriced almond milk latte (and yes, I posted a picture of it, don't you know who I am?!). All around me, people are hurrying in and out, a passing blur of rush-rush-rush. Many of them dash inside, grab their usual, and run right out, down the block and out of view. In the street, ten Prius cars (question: Is the plural form of Prius *Prii*?) go zooming by. A dazed and confused woman nearly bikes into oncoming traffic because she's not paying attention. Another man sprints down the street during a green light, dodging between cars before his parking meter expires.

I lose count of the people scurrying along, heads down, engrossed in their smartphones, typing out messages, doubtlessly answering an email that "can't wait" (though it most likely can), or posting something on social media with equally unnecessary urgency.

And all of this is unfolding before my very eyes on an average day, begging the question: *WHY. IS. EVERYONE. IN. SUCH. A. DAMN. HURRY?* Why the constant rush? Why are people always running late? Who will die if that email isn't answered in moving traffic? Can't we sit down, breathe, and enjoy a minor pause for, like, two minutes? I just don't get it. I, someone whose entire world revolves around all the things that are grinding my gears, just can't understand when we all became so . . . so . . . *this*!

I feel as though time has increasingly become like currency in today's world, and everyone around me seems to be going broke, spending it at warp speed. A mass poverty of patience is leading to everyone giving less attention to the things that really matter: being present in the moment, actively participating in social interactions without distractions from our devices, and actually *listening* to one another. *Really* listening. Our busyness—or rather, our perception of busyness—is a form of self-robbery that drives me crazy.

"I've been trying to schedule dinner with my friend for weeks," a friend said to me one afternoon. "My BEST friend, and she keeps saying that she's too busy with work. She can't give up one evening, and it sucks."

"I don't know this girl personally," I responded, shaking my head and pursing my lips. "But 'too busy' is a damn lie. Everyone is busy. Everyone has work to do. But there are twenty-four hours in a day. Yes, work is important, and yes, it's inevitable that a large chunk of our time gets chewed up by our professional obligations, but I'll guarantee this: the 168 hours everyone is given every week are not being fully utilized. She needs to work out her priorities."

Granted, I was probably being a little judgmental/semi-cynical, but I find modern schedules to be exhausting. And how ironic is that? I'm the most millennial person I know. *chuckles to self*

In being so connected these days—morning, noon, and night—I think we've all adopted a sense of urgency around everything we do. Answer that email now! Share that post now! Jump on the call now! Do it now. Now. Now. Now. *Now!* Otherwise, we fear we'll miss out or get left behind.

The world seems to move at an alarming rate nowadays. There I go saying "nowadays" again. (*Ugh*, I swear I'm not a grandpa wearing a mask, pretending to be a twenty-four-year-old. I SWEAR. *edit and save*) Meals can be delivered to us in seconds, everything is now payable via the swipe of a plastic card or the tap of a smartphone, work hours seem to bleed into free time, and we all can be reached at any hour of the day because we can't seem to put down our technology for more than a second. *Ugh*. That list alone stresses me out. But it's reality. We now live in a world of "GO, GO, GO" instead of "Let's cook a nice family meal, sit down, *talk* about our feelings, and communicate as a family/friends." You know, like we did twenty years ago. (Oh gosh, I'm old enough to remember what life was like twenty years ago! Someone call my therapist—I feel a quarter-life crisis coming on . . . again.)

To validate this, I asked my friends what life was like when they were growing up, compared to what it's like now. "Did you eat family meals together?" or "Do you ever turn your phone off and just not look at it for the night?" Most said that over the years, they've noticed a gradual decline in personal time spent with their loved ones. They accept that they've fallen to their knees at the behest of technology, choosing to watch television or swipe through their devices during meals instead of engaging with the people around them. Most people I know appear to find it genuinely hard to unplug, due to the fear of missing something important. It's sad because I feel the same way. As much as I can point this out, I'm as guilty of it as the next person. It's a difficult habit to break.

Our devices are walls we carry around with us. We erect them inside the home, around restaurant tables, in the car, and even at concerts! These devices are meant to connect us, but in some ways they're barriers to communication and connection, especially with the people we spend our real lives with. That's why I'm making more of a concerted effort to carve out space for myself . . . and my friends. In that space, in unplugging from my technology dependency and refusing to cite the "too busy" excuse, I have discovered more light-bulb moments, realizations, and helpful insights about myself and the world around me. It's almost like I'm dating myself and, in order to get to know me better, I need to spend more unplugged time with me. I like to think that this is how I'll grow: by stepping out of the blur and into more clarity.

It's crazy what you'll see, hear, and feel if you stop and let the world continue to move around you for even just a minute. Right now, as I sit here writing in this café, a song is playing that I've never heard before. Through the window, I notice the sun has begun to set, turning the clouds that orangey-pink color I really like. The girl sitting next to me is also writing in what seems to be a journal. Another girl to my right is sitting there, looking out the window with a completely blank stare, as though contemplating something deep and personal. She looks reflective, in a sad way. I hope she's okay! Speaking of okay, I wonder if my friends back home are? I haven't talked to them in a couple weeks. I'd better give them a call to check in. Yup, I need to do more of that, too.

Basically, I'm trying to pay attention. I mean, I have to force myself to do it through fits of angst, but the fire has been lit and here I am: trying to be mindful of my surroundings and the people around me. Noting the detail. Ignoring my phone. Thinking beyond my next appointment. I invite you to give it a try right now. This is the only time I'm going to tell you to put down my book (no matter how incredible you're finding this piece of literature) and be in the moment with yourself for a few minutes. Try it. I hope you'll feel calmer and more observant. The world will keep going. The planet will keep revolving. Life will go on. But along the way, even when feeling harried or overwhelmed, try to remember to take a little time out . . . for others, and for you. No one's going to force you; only you can. But who am I to tell you what to do? I don't know. All I know is I'm going to stop writing now and call my friends.

greed & desire

how naive are we
to conceive thoughts
and beliefs
that a world which gives
while we only receive
owes more
to our wants
and needs

oh, how i pity us

you can't lose what you never had to begin with

My bedroom used to be lined with windows, which was lovely during the daytime but was very much the opposite in the early hours of the morning when the rising sun tried to break through. (Conveniently, all the windows were covered with white wooden shutters.)

On March 17, 2014, around 9 a.m., I was in bed, sleeping away. I'm not sure what I was dreaming about; all I remember is that my dream began to get fuzzy, almost shaky. No, wait, I was *literally* shaking. Before even opening my eyes, I heard the clanking of the wooden shutters as my entire room moved up and down. I was jolted forward, and I opened my eyes in total confusion, drenched in sweat. "What's happening? Am I dreaming, or is this real life?"

After what seemed like a few minutes but was probably only seconds, the shaking ended. It just stopped. I soon discovered I had experienced an earthquake—my first earthquake, in fact. And in that moment, when my bedroom rocked like a boat, shaking back and forth with no warning, I realized something: I have no control. None. Nada. *Nothing.* The world was shaking and I couldn't do a thing to stop it. With that realization, it was as if a lightbulb magically lit up above my sweaty forehead. I can't control *anything.* Things like this will happen regardless of whether I want them to or not. No notes of consideration will be sent to my door.

I probably should have had a mental breakdown at that point, but I lay back in bed and quickly live-tweeted my first earthquake experience. (Some things never change . . .)

One thing I've always struggled with in my life is dealing with the uncontrollable. If you know me, then this is pretty obvious (*chuckles under his breath*). Whether it's an unexpectedly long line, being picked fifth when I feel like I should've been first, rain on a day I want to spend outside, or a friend canceling plans at the last minute—it's all beyond me. Life is an infinite loop of uncontrollable events. We wake up to them, we fall asleep to them, we're powerless to stop them, and we fall to our knees at their whim. It's just how it is. But you know what? That's okay.

Before your mind goes to, *Well* someone *has control issues,* I'll stop you right there. (Also, how dare you??)

Ever since I was a kid, one of my favorite things has been to have a schedule. (I'm actually laughing out loud as I type this.) It's not that I love to be in control; it's more that it freaks me out how much control we DON'T have. When you think about it, we can't regulate anything outside ourselves, and, to be honest, we can't even regulate ourselves. We live in that infinite loop, and there is no other choice but to find peace with it.

Like I said, I've never been good with the unknown, but the older I get, the more I realize that this is how it's always going to be. If I truly want to fret less and live freely, I need to stop being such a worrywart! (That. Phrase. Is. Disgusting.)

With age comes responsibility, and with responsibility comes an acceptance of uncertainty, especially as each of us moves blindly through the darkness of adulthood. (It's not that dark, but again, I love being dramatic!)

One thing I'm continually reminded of is the truth that I don't know, um, shit. Listen, I like to think I'm a pretty intelligent, switched-on human being, but there are a thousand more things I don't know anything about than things I do. But the beauty of existence is the journey from beginning to end. Along the way, I might learn about those one thousand things. I hope I do! I can only endeavor to move forward and learn and grow in my knowledge of the world. Beyond that intention, there's not much more I can do. It's the same for all of us. We need to trust the greater unknown, throw our cards in the air, and deal with wherever they fall.

Today, I was in line at the airport, waiting to go through security. It was a typical Sunday morning in sunny Los Angeles, without a cloud in the sky, and my Uber driver played the right music all the way there. In real life, the people in this city are relatively laid-back and keep to themselves. Welllll, not at the airport.

Airports are a real-life peek into what (I'm assuming) hell looks like. They're gross, loud, and if I'm being honest, horribly run and downright uncomfortable (much like hell). Airports suck, and that day, I was stuck in one.

After being dropped off, I rounded the corner of the terminal to approach the security area and was immediately confronted with the sickening sight of a massive line. Gross. No. Anything but WAITING!

Admittedly, I have come to expect such things. I never go anywhere and think the journey will be smooth. (I'll leave such expectations for the happily naive.) There will forever be unexpected complications along every pathway.

As I joined the slithering monstrosity that was the security line, the voices around me grew sharp and dissonant.

"Can this line move any SLOWER?" said a man with a briefcase.

"This is ridiculous. I'll be reporting this!" said a child in a suit with a rewards card.

"I can't believe they're making us STAND this long!" said a lady in (stunning) six-inch heels.

I'm hungry. Will there be donuts on the other side? said my inner voice.

I began to giggle to myself. Who are these people? What throne do they sit on? IT'S A FREAKIN' LINE, NOT THE END OF THE WORLD. No one can do anything about this, so why are they complaining as if they can? It's totally and completely out of our control. Why waste the energy? We're all going to get through when we get through, and that's how it is. Relax. There's no way to avoid this. Maybe write a passive-aggressive tweet about it if you have to.

It's in moments like this that I feel proud of myself. Like, so damn proud. Because I'm learning. I'm practicing what I preach. I'm not losing my mind over lost time, and I feel good about it. It's in situations like this that I almost freeze-frame the world, step out of my body, look around, acknowledge that there's nothing I can do to affect the outcome, shrug, jump back into my body, breathe, and wait patiently. And that pause works for me. After a few minutes, the line moved painfully slowly, but I made it to my gate with more than enough time to spare. And nobody died from waiting in an unexpectedly long line! WOW. Who knew!

All right, I make this mental feat of acceptance sound easy, and it's also a horrible, first-world problem to overcome, but I think you get the point. It only just happened to me, so yay for immediate inspiration! TAKE THAT, PROCRASTINATION! I'M WRITING IT DOWN. Ha!

For me, the key to this acceptance is all about taking a pause and assessing your situation from a clear mental space. I can only recommend that you try it. Instead of becoming flustered or stressed about a delay or a time-sensitive situation, ask yourself this: "Can I do anything to fix this?" No? Okay then. Wait, breathe, and, nine times out of ten, it will fix itself. Note to self: it pays to be patient. Your mom was right!

Now, here's some real talk: Most of us will never fully be able to accept that we have no control. Most of us like to labor under the idea that we are in control of our environments, and maybe we are, to a certain extent. But when events outside of our control start to unfold, we can always remind ourselves of the true situation. Trust me, it works: Close your eyes and whisper to yourself, "This is out of my control, and it will be okay." Tell yourself that until you believe every word. You can't fix what has already been messed up. Sometimes— well, most times—you need to roll with life's punches and let go. Just let it go.

misplaced organs

Your brain might frequently speak with uncertainty, but your heart will lead you to your truth. It's so true. Which is why I'm increasingly starting to think with my heart more than my head. *Wait,* you say. *How do you think with the heart?* Especially in a world where we are told, usually by parents or teachers, to "use that thing on your shoulders!" or "You were born with a brain for a reason!"

While I don't dispute that, I also maintain that we were given a heart for a reason (aside from the whole "It keeps us alive" thing): to feel our way through life. I'm not even sure we're meant to think our way through our days, ongoing problems, and big-picture issues. The mind is there to weigh options, to process the pros and cons, and to filter thoughts in the moment. But real decision-making, for me, is best conducted through the heart. Before I make a big decision, I ask myself: is my heart into the idea? I let my heart "think" it through . . . and feel what's right.

Now, don't get me wrong, I use my brain a lot. *gasp* I consider it one of the most important tools any human can wield. But I consider my heart's opinion first. My mind is full of uncertainty—always has been, always will be. It questions everything and turns situations inside out, based on my preexisting knowledge and past experiences. But the mind can be so busy, buzzing with information, and it can easily get lost. Clouds can roll through my own mind at the drop of a hat, and those accumulations can fog my judgment and potential decision-making. I'm not here for that ambiguity. I'm not here for that one bit. But the heart speaks truth with crystal clarity. It somehow knows the answers to life's most difficult obstacles. I don't know how; it just does. And most importantly, I trust it. Trust is what determines my preference for the heart over the mind. I don't trust my mind because it has so many filters (and contains way too many rabbit holes and avenues that lead to me chasing, or fretting over, false thoughts). It has an erratic tendency to play games with me and invent worries and fears and illusions that don't turn out to be true or have any basis in fact. The heart is different. It's pure. Unfiltered. Unbiased. It knows nothing but fact. There is only one reality for it to face and only one light in the path of darkness. The heart is naturally wise.

Admittedly, it's scary to trust an organ that modern culture sometimes paints as less reliable than the brain, but that organ literally keeps us breathing, existing. I don't know about you, but I follow it like my North Star. I willingly fall at the mercy of my emotions that shift the needle of this compass within me. I listen to what it says. Really listen. I hear its whisper and its roar. What is it telling me?

lingering shadows

9:31 p.m.

for the longest time there was a shadow
lingering over us like a cloud above a city
we avoided it like an illness, fleeing to
the mountains in search of the sun
but there was only rain
and we could only run
so far

i was in love

Today, my heart got stepped on. "Stepped on." *Ha.* Scratch that. Who am I kidding? On this very day, my heart was ripped out, thrown on the ground, jumped on, smooshed, trampled, and smudged into the earth. Ground into the dirt. At least, that's how it feels. I feel weird writing about this, but I need to work myself through it a little. I'm going to open up for a bit with little to no filter, so please be kind . . .

My two-year relationship ended right before my eyes, and there was nothing, I repeat, NOTHING I could do about it; it was a bit like being a witness to a car crash played out in slow motion. You know it's happening, you brace for the impact, then pray the damage will be minimal, even though you know otherwise. You *know.*

Yes, that's what it feels like. But before I go any deeper, let me backtrack to shed light on how I got here in the first place.

Being a closeted gay individual for most of my teenage years and early adulthood has drastically shaped my outlook on love, sex, and relationships. Growing up, I watched everyone around me feel this "love" thing on a daily basis. *Young love*, as it's referred to. I never got to experience that. I never developed crushes like my friends did. Well, I did, but these "crushes" were forced. I remember being very aware of how boys and girls were supposed to like each other, so, up until I was twenty, and on a yearly basis, I persuaded myself to *feel* just an ounce of an emotional connection to girls. And I was consistently successful! Well, it depends on how you define *success*, but I was able to develop some level of feeling for a few girls over the years, even managing to convince everyone around me. *Score. Crushed it.* But I was lying to myself and the poor girls I was dating, causing them unexpected heartbreak for no real reason. I just "wasn't feeling it" because, well, I wasn't.

On each occasion, I remember feeling so bad about how quickly I would get over them. *I feel nothing*, I constantly thought. Obviously, my feelings were fake, completely fabricated so I could be "normal," even if for only a brief moment in time. As a result, my ideas about love were messed up and became warped over the years. Frankly, I slowly began to believe that love wasn't a real thing. If I didn't feel it, could it really exist? I wasn't sure. I felt only emptiness, a black hole inside my heart, a wormhole into nothingness. *Maybe everyone else is faking it?* I thought. *Maybe I'm programmed wrong. Maybe I'm not meant to feel such things.* In fact, I had pretty much resigned myself to this outcome, telling myself that I'd better get used to it. *I must be broken. I keep trying and the result is always the same. I MUST be broken* . . . I'd think as I lay in bed in my blankets and tears. That was a cycle I found myself in for years.

Until 2014. That's when I began the process of accepting my sexuality and stayed on the path to becoming open about it (in my own circles and in my own time). I started to slowly comprehend what it could be like to love someone. *I could love another guy!* I started to think. *Hell, I can see myself* marrying *a guy.* It might not sound like it, but that was a breakthrough—a quantum leap in my mind, especially after having thought that love and marriage could only be between a man and a woman. And yet, I still struggled to see how I could be with another guy permanently, how I could love him, truly. Because, again, for all intents and purposes, I still didn't know what love even felt like. There's a huge difference between wanting to be with another person and wanting to spend your life with that person—the difference between a crush and love. "Forever" gradually becomes a possibility in your mind that you are more than okay with. BUT. How. Could. I. Do. That? My brain just didn't get it . . . until it did.

I can't pinpoint the exact moment in time when I realized I was falling in love, but my move to California had a lot to do with it. Once immersed in an openly gay environment, I quickly understood that men loving men (and women loving women) was normal. It was BEAUTIFUL, in fact. The spectrum of love made my eyes widen with adoration and appreciation. I'm a very visual person, you see. And let's just say in West Hollywood, you see *a lot* of gay people. They're everywhere, unashamedly being true to who they are, and who they love. It was the single most refreshing thing to witness. To this very day, when I see an openly gay couple in public, it makes my heart flutter and warms every inch of my being, brightening my soul in ways I can't begin to describe. Those couples became a symbol of hope to me, and to see them firsthand made me think it was possible for me to be like them. To love. To be happy. It was *actually* possible to dream of the future. The future I wanted to have.

Now, I know you want me to get back to how this justifiably dramatic passage began, but hang in there, sweet human. You see, before you can know heartbreak, you must have someone break your heart. And in late 2014, I set myself up for that. I fell in love hard. I fell as fast as the sun seems to set: slowly, then quickly, then all at once.

The spark was there, the colors burst as bright as can be, and my head was over my heels before I knew it. That's when I got it. I suddenly understood what love is. What it COULD be. It was actually a real thing, and it blew my mind. Turns out, the overused cliché is true: *When you know, you know.* The feeling is undeniable. The butterflies come by the thousands. The excitement feels like electricity. I couldn't stop smiling, hard as I tried. Something inside of me ignited. When together with your loved one, you're flying. When apart, all you wish is to be together. It's the only thing you can think about. Honestly, I could go on and on about this feeling of elation, but I think you get it. Some force that I didn't think existed now had me in its very real grip. I was in love. Now, I share a lot of aspects of my life with the world, from what I had for breakfast (eggs over easy) to the ridiculous text my dad just sent ("I think I butt-dialed you twice HA"). I'm very open. But one of the main things I rarely talk about is relationships in any form, whether it's with friends, family, or a boy. That's the boundary I've drawn for myself. Some things deserve to be kept private, personal, and wholeheartedly to myself. I reserve that right and am thankful that people, for the most part, respect it.

In keeping with that philosophy, I'll withhold specific details here, but that doesn't mean I can't share what I'm feeling right this very second. I'm experiencing a feeling that I've never felt before; it's the feeling—the risk—that comes with love, and it's the worst: heartbreak. Unfortunately, heartbreak isn't unique—it's universal. It's a vulnerability that we all experience and understand, or will one day come to understand.

My heart is broken. After two years, countless shared experiences, endless secrets, and giving all of myself . . . I am crushed. And it feels like the closest thing to being destroyed that I've ever known, and I feel as if I'm beyond repair. I feel alone. I *am* alone. I haven't been alone in two fucking years, and I don't even know how to be this anymore. It's like I've forgotten what it was like before, and now I'm being forced to remember when I don't want to remember. *Ugh*, that sucks. Even as I type these words in the corner of a local coffee shop, I'm shaking, choking back the tears, resisting the urge to have a complete emotional breakdown. My hands are tense. I kind of want to vomit. Fuck, this is the worst.

The hardest part is that I knew this was coming. I'm young; he's young. So I guess it was inevitable, right? According to all the stories, "young love doesn't last." They say there's so much love out there in the world that we should experience a little of it before settling down. I don't know about that. Just because that's how it is for a lot of people doesn't mean that's how it must be for everyone, right? Apparently not. As hard as I tried, and as much as I gave of myself, it wasn't enough to make this relationship last. I can't point fingers or make excuses, and I can't go any further because I don't want to make anyone out to be a villain, but these emotions—these new and powerful emotions—are messing with my mind. I don't know what to think or believe. As I sit here right now, I don't know. I just don't know . . . anything.

I never knew a person could feel this way. Just like the once foreign feeling of love, I didn't know pain like this existed. This. Fucking. Sucks. I'll repeat that until you believe it: This. Fucking. SUCKS. But this, *too*, is love. As much as people talk about love, you also hear about heartbreak constantly; to be honest, you probably hear about it more. Pain is the other side of the same coin. It is both the presence and the absence of love; the residual feeling when the physical relationship is over, lingering like a stinging wound that won't close up. Not that any of this makes me feel better. My world is flipped upside down, and I don't know where to run, even though every fiber of my being is telling me *RUN. GET OUT OF HERE. RUN AWAY.*

I imagine that this is what it feels like to unknowingly be in a life-threatening situation. You don't understand why, but your mind is screaming at you to stop doing what you're doing. Something isn't right and you need to stop it, now, before something bad happens. Love must trigger a similar fight-or-flight burst of adrenaline. All I want to do is flee back to the past, to stop what is happening now and figure out a way to go back to yesterday. *How can I stop this? What can I do to fix it? There must be something. Anything. This is a dream. This isn't real. This can't be happening. Everything was fine two hours ago. How could this happen? How could I let this happen? How did YOU let this happen?*

You did this. You did this. Come back and fix it.

Please.

I know I'm talking irrationally, but I can't seem to be any other way. This must be what it's like to feel crazy. It's so strange. I feel incapable of doing what I need to do to pull myself together in this moment. I haven't told anyone this has happened yet. Once I talk about it, then it becomes true. Maybe if I ignore my sadness, it'll go away? Maybe if I pretend for long enough that this isn't happening, I'll wake up next to him and it will have been only a nightmare . . .

Okay, I thought it would be therapeutic to write down my feelings in this hyperemotional state, but explaining it only seems to be making things worse. It's not helping in the way I had hoped. I wonder if anything will help. Is that possible? I've . . . I've never been here before. And I never want to be here again.

I can't stop thinking that he and I will never do anything together again. "We" doesn't exist anymore. "We" are now separate people. And it's that separation that feels unbearable.

I'm sorry, I can't write about this anymore. I need to be alone for a while and just . . . cry. Maybe that will help until I fall asleep. The pain subsides when I sleep.

Fuck. I'm sad. Sorry for the downer.

I'll be fine.

Eventually.

broken

*i am broken up
after being
broken up with*

too hopeful for my own good

5:25 p.m.

today my heart was ripped in two
one half for me, one half for you
take a half and keep it near
i have mine and will always be here
crossing paths before the end
once a lover, forever a friend

i hope you know i still admire you
i hope you know i still desire you

i am
a ruin
ruined
by
another

seconds

9:36 p.m.

it must hurt
to know i was your first everything
for everything now
is sloppy seconds

it will always be okay

I've never been a big fan of attending awards shows. Most are pretentious, and few are truly entertaining. In theory, it sounds fun to witness the glamour and chaos of the red carpet firsthand. But the truth is that once you're done up, looking fine, and immersed in such superficial gatherings . . . it's not all that. The novelty soon wears thin.

I don't know. Maybe that's just me.

Regardless, here I am, sitting in the Staples Center (capacity: roughly 20,000) as a guest at the fifty-eighth annual Grammy Awards—THE night in the music world. And yet I'm not excited to be here. In fact, I'm pretty uncomfortable. After several hours—yes, this show goes on for HOURS—I just can't take it anymore.

In fairness to the Grammys, it's not their fault. I can't blame this on Kanye, either. No, I'm struggling for personal reasons, as explained in the previous chapter, and I have to leave in the least dramatic way possible before I have an emotional meltdown. So, I get up, say my good-byes, and make a silent exit (because let's be real, no one cared that I was there anyway).

The fresh air helps a bit, but I still want to go home so I can have a good cry and let it all out. I order a car, and a short while later, a middle-aged man swoops curbside and picks me up.

Sure enough, only a few minutes into the journey, I totally lose it.

Tears begin falling from my face and my nose stuffs up; if I could look in a mirror, I'm sure I would resemble a person suffering a horrendous allergic reaction. Before I know it, my quiet weeping transitions into loud sobbing . . . and I can't stop. My sadness doesn't seem to care that I'm dissolving in the back of some stranger's car.

And that's when he, the driver, begins to hand tissues to me over his shoulder. He doesn't break his concentration on the road. Not once. He simply continues to pass me fresh tissues with his right hand, keeping his left on the steering wheel without even glancing at me in the rearview mirror, as deftly and nonchalantly as a magician pulling out a never-ending handkerchief from his sleeve.

As he does, my mind plays games with me, repeatedly whispering insecure, heartbreak-induced words in my ear, like *worthless*, *pathetic*, and *pointless*. In the midst of my sadness, I believe everything I'm saying to myself, and it makes me feel even more horrible. I try my hardest to focus on the music playing in the car, hoping it drowns out the words in my head.

After a solid forty-five minutes of driving (fuck this Los Angeles traffic!) and another half dozen tissues later, we pull up outside of my house. I'm a total wreck at this point, and there's no trying to hide it. "Thanks . . . so much . . . for . . . the ride," I say, in between sobs and sniffles, trying not to sound like a total mess.

The driver hands me another tissue and finally looks at me, totally composed. And he says, "Sir, whatever is upsetting you, just know that it will be okay. It will always be okay." He says it so gently, so sincerely. His kindness in that moment—his understanding and empathy—makes me want to bawl even more. I can barely utter "thank you," to the extent that my gratitude comes out as a whisper.

I step out of the car and he drives away, turning the corner at the end of my street and vanishing into the night. I sit on my steps and continue my pity party for one. But the truth is that I don't stop thinking about what the driver said to me. His words didn't cure me then and there, but I would remember them in the days ahead. Because it *will* be okay. It will always be okay.

I just needed the kindness of a stranger to remind me of that.

sometimes even the worst dreams are better

than this reality

a mind at its worst

forgettable

worthless

pointless

useless

expendable

i am none of the above

stop tricking me into

thinking otherwise

please stop

please

her peach sunglasses

People don't realize the daily power they have to make others happy. All it takes is a few kind words, delivered without expectation. It's not much, honestly. Giving someone a compliment or slight encouragement is the one thing *any* of us can do, at any time. It's free, it's easy, and, boy, can it do the world wonders.

For some reason, I've always felt uncomfortable talking to strangers in any capacity. I'm the type of guy who will mentally rehearse his dinner order at a restaurant until I have to say it out loud to the server. *Don't fuck this up, Connor! You. Have. One. Shot. DON'T FUCK THIS UP!!* Nine times out of ten, I stutter or stumble over my words and everything goes to shit, but who's counting? (Me.)

I'm getting better at it now because, frankly, it's my job. I've been honing my social skills and public-speaking abilities over the past three years due to the industry I find myself in. It has thrust me into situations that have ripped me out of my comfort zone and taught me confidence. I meet countless people who do every job imaginable, so in a way, my life is like one giant speed-dating session and, whether I like it or not, I'm deathly single. I have to meet them all because who knows if I'll find a match made in work heaven! (I don't think I'm making sense or am even close to a metaphor at this point, so . . . LET'S MOVE ON.)

The other day I was out and about with a few friends, walking down Melrose Avenue in Los Angeles, browsing shops and store windows, as we do. A group of girls was walking toward us in the opposite direction, and I quickly noticed how cool one of them looked. She had this cute, short haircut that still maintained some waves, and she wore baggy jeans with a tucked-in, white graphic tee, complete with a pair of round, peach-colored sunglasses. My description doesn't do her outfit justice, but she was cute as hell and everyone could tell.

Now, I could do one of two things here: 1) not say a thing, or 2) say a thing. It's simple. Those were my options. I'm willing to bet most people would go with option one and move along, perhaps feeling a slight twinge of regret for not having the guts to say something. I used to be that way, but with practice, I now adopt the "why not?" attitude. What's so hard about telling people they look great? (In the least "I'm hitting on you" way possible, of course.) If done correctly, with sincerity and no weirdness intended, nothing can go wrong.

As this girl approached us, I made eye contact, smiled, and spoke up. "Hey, you're killing it. You look great!"

She looked surprised. "Oh, thank you?!" she said, as if no one had ever paid her a compliment before (which I highly doubt because style like that could NOT be an accident). I continued smiling, nodded in acknowledgment of her response, and kept walking on with my friends.

I thought something, and wasn't going to hold back from sharing that honest thought. In doing so, it actually left *me* feeling like a million bucks, and, judging by the look on her face, she felt a similar sensation of giddiness. It felt good to make someone else feel good about herself. Apparently, the giving and receiving of a compliment has mutual benefits. Who knew?

In a world that appears to indulge in negativity, I find we need to do our best to share the good. Too many shows, blogs, and newspapers spew pessimism, seemingly dedicated to tearing people down and picking them apart, piece by piece, until there's nothing left. This horribly judgmental trend has no point, save for spite and harm. You merely have to flick through magazines or scroll through the online entertainment sites to observe how people's fashion, hair, bodies, and even personalities are being dissected for commentary. Spend five minutes on Twitter and you'll see a constant stream of pointless, vitriolic trolling every time you refresh your feed. It's sad. It's sad to me when it's not even *about* me. Rarely does anyone have anything nice to say anymore. It's a playground of sore shut-ins bitching and gossiping, where people drag others down for their own twisted entertainment. And the danger of this online activity is that it spills over into real life. You can't fake hatred like that. Thankfully, kind Uber drivers who pass me tissues are my reassuring reminder that goodness and kindness remain in abundance out there. Good people do exist, even if most of them are not known to the wider public and live their lives under the radar.

We have enough badness in the real world without adding to it in the virtual one, and we need to remember that we're capable of projecting goodness. We need to spread love, kindness, and empathy to the masses. At the end of the day, we're all humans, with hang-ups and unknown struggles and insecurities we face daily, silently. Think about that, and be aware that we are *all* this way. It's not just you and not just me. Everyone has baggage. Pause for a second and think of something nice to say instead of indulging in pointless negativity.

So, next time you see someone who's wearing something cool or dope or unique, or maybe got a new haircut or hair color, acknowledge it. Show that you noticed it in the way the person wanted to be noticed, be it a friend, relative, or total stranger. I'm not sure there's anything better than being noticed. And you watch: the more you do it, the more the kindness will spread out like a ripple. Trust me on this: you'll walk a little taller for simply speaking up, no strings attached, no ifs, ands, or buts.

you

9:27 p.m.

your smell and smile
could make even the strongest
fall to their knees

better days

in those moments
we are overcome with feeling
warmly embraced by fate
the soft kiss of no expectations
a greeting of peace
a message of hope
sweet serenity
leaks from pore and palm
nothing can go wrong
everything is right
i

am

okay

frames

photographs fly down
where we used to lie down
removed by the same hands
that used to hold my hands
together we pack them away
in cardboard capsules
behind closed doors
memories stay and decay
in the grace of queens and kings
to a land where dreams are made
now hidden in darkness
an empty row of nails line the wall
my eyes sting with pain
his white tee stained
with a cocktail of tears
we wish to hide beside them
two stowaways capsized in the present
below our melted hearts
blood drains from our veins
as the door closes one last time
on everything we used to know
our eyes shut before midnight
no words to break the silence
wishing for an extra hour
hoping for a better day
like the ones depicted
behind the wooden frames

an unmemorable day
made memorable

I t's crazy how I can remember a specific day from the now-distant past so vividly. A day in which nothing super-significant happened, except for the fact that it was just, well, a really good day. My recall of a day shared with you—a special someone—is almost cinematic. Take this snapshot as an example:

I woke up at the right time, feeling refreshed, not at all groggy after a damn near stirless sleep, with only your smile to greet mine in the morning as we stretched and rolled around in the messy covers. The sheets were warm; the air remained a little cold. A happy dream lingered in my mind, my face reflecting its quickly fading memory, making me smile. I rolled out of bed and headed to the kitchen to brew up a couple of coffees before snuggling on the couch with mug in hand and you by my side. My calendar was clear; all usual commitments were nonexistent. The day was ours, for you and me alone to fill with whatever our hearts desired.

Outside, the weather was cool enough to wear a jacket, so I grabbed a favorite from the closet and we held hands as we walked to the bookstore. There, we enjoyed another coffee before sharing literary finds with each other, comparing choices that were so fitting and inappropriately appropriate. We observed the passing pedestrians and kissed behind bookcases. We grabbed a light lunch of avo' on toast with another coffee—because that's about as crazy as we got. We swung on the swings in a nearby park like the kids we were. The clouds were sprinkled lightly across the sky in a way that added to the sense of peace. You talked. I listened. Nothing important was said, but all the words were open and spoken with ease, bringing questions and giggles in between.

And there was that smile. That goddamn smile that made my knees weak. When I was able to make it appear, I couldn't help but feel excited. I couldn't help but feel closer than the eye can see. The hours ticked by, to the extent that we lost the sense of time that we never truly had on this good day. And then we made our way home, not because we had to but because we wanted to.

Joined by friends and family, the warmth of togetherness slowly grew, continuing into the night; we were a little community watching TV shows, perfectly imperfect in all the right ways. The conversation was alive, and the contagious happiness was like ecstasy in the air that made everyone glow. Then, just like that, it was time for this day to end where it began: with our heads on the pillow, cuddling and sleeping with the smallest, most content of smiles. We had no fears that day. No worries. We were carefree. It was nice to merely exist— to be—and existing had never felt so light.

That one ordinary, unremarkable day became memorable purely for being good.

Let's never forget our good days; we should string them together like pearls on a necklace, to be treasured and remembered whenever days don't make us feel as good. I think that sometimes it's the memory of simple, ordinary, happy days that sustains us. The ones without expectation, that come with no strings attached. The ones that stand out for blending in, and can be appreciated for that reason alone.

What a good day that was.

bloodshot

3:01 a.m.

when i lie awake
long enough for the clock
to tick over to a new day
my heart beats faster
as i begin to question
what brings worth to living
the scariest moment comes
when my eyes remain open
through an hour
empty of answers

arguments in antemeridian

8:53 a.m.

the rain came again
the morning was left cold
we used to argue about these times
so playful and lighthearted.
today, i guess i got my way
but would give anything for you to get yours

morning silence

Do you know what I appreciate? Morning silence. When I'm up and awake before anyone else. When the sun has just risen and sends shimmering beams of gold through the window, drenching my home in light. When I'm walking around, trying to be as weightless as a feather but the floorboards still manage to emit a slight creak or two.

From outside, the sound of an occasional passing car momentarily interrupts the quiet of daybreak, but I hear it almost as a greeting. "Hello, fellow early riser. How do you do? Where are you off to?" And then, another window of silence is broken by a bird chirping ever so softly amongst the palms outside—nature's alarm clock, I guess. A distant voice is heard from across the street—doubtless a duo of walkers getting some exercise before rushing off to work. The street is beginning to stir and this moment is coming to an end.

As the rest of the city slowly wakes, the air is cooler than usual, so I wrap myself up in a blanket, cocooned in comfort and immediate warmth. In the kitchen, the coffee begins to drip, and each drip invites me to get up and get going. Everything is perfectly in its place from the previous day. All things lie in their natural state, as if frozen overnight.

The sun gleams through, seemingly brighter than before. *It's going to be a good one*, I think as I pour the first of many cups of coffee. I have no reason to know that, but I sense the goodness in the air.

I take my first sip, and my mind hums. Yes. Welcome to your new day, a day that started in sublime stillness.

up at 5 a.m.

i can feel every eyelash, every itch, every breath that i take

i'm wide awake

thinking about you

and i don't know how to stop

i saw a boy in larchmont

a familiar face
of the one i once knew
sends me to the floor
amid the clatter of coffee cups
the voices of strangers
in a place i thought safe
a haven turned traitor
only my eyes lift to meet you
for the first time in eight or nine
old wounds return new
somehow deeper than before
escape, my mind whispers
you're in danger
you need to run
run far from here
in any direction
with any destination
the whisper now turned siren
alarmed though there's no real threat
cautious nonetheless
startled by my past
fearful of my future
setting me back all those months
running faster now
crying harder now
the boy in larchmont
tilts back into my nightmares
as i flee down the street
who knew a sight
once seen daily
could make eyes
this sore
again

excuses, excuses

we will forever

find excuses

not to

but you only need

one reason

to

runaway

It's late May, the seasons are changing, and I'm off again, headed as far away as I can stand to go on my own. Honestly, the destination couldn't matter less at this point. All that matters is that I get away.

I figure that if I flee as soon as things aren't working, then maybe I'll be all right. Maybe everything will become good again if I run away to somewhere better. By going to a new location on a new day in a new time zone filled with new people and new experiences, maybe, just maybe, everything will turn out better. Maybe.

This isn't my first dramatic escape. If it were, I would be much more frightened and damn near crippled with anxiety. This is, however, my first time leaving the country to do it. I've never fled so far. Typically, I'll go somewhere like the Northwest to visit my brother (did that twice) or home to Minnesota to be in the comfort of my parents' home (did that twice as well) or to New York to get caught up in the busy city life surrounded by strangers, but hey, at least I'm not alone (did that once). But never before have I gone as far as London. That's quite excessive, especially from Los Angeles: eleven hours by plane, five thousand miles away, eight hours "into the future." That's, um, a lot. Even for me.

As per usual, I've convinced myself that I'm leaving for a good reason: to be with friends, or to take some time off, or simply because I want to. Sadly, those are lies—deep-rooted lies told to myself and everyone close to me. They're all bullshit excuses that further distance myself from the truth. Deep down, only I know I'm running away. Nothing feels right, or the same, or good at "home" in Los Angeles anymore. It's shit, continues to be shit, and I need to get away from this shit. I need to leave behind the constant reminders of what was and what will never be. I have to escape the pain that bombards me from every direction and haunts my mind with lingering questions. I'm sore from thinking, and my senses are numb to reality. It's not even about a broken heart anymore. I'm back to where I was in college, reverting to the depression that cripples my everyday existence. Everything is shit or, at least, that's what the depression convinces me is true. It's like looking into a foggy mirror that won't clear up. No matter how many times I try to wipe it away, the haze returns.

In a way, this is my version of fight versus flight. I'm not a fighter, as you might very well know. I hate confrontation in any form and avoid it like the plague. But I do fly when the going gets tough. Literally. I jump on a plane and it seems to work . . . for a while. It makes things better . . . for a few days. But I soon learn that none of these trips really help. I quickly become engulfed in the fog once again. These trips don't fix me; they don't stop my hive of a mind from buzzing day in and day out. But, alas, I'm an optimist at heart, and I'm hoping that this trip to London will be the one that defies the rest. And so here I sit in Delta economy at Los Angeles International Airport, running away, hoping the fourth time's a charm.

The first time I ran, I genuinely believed it would help in a significant way. After booking my ticket, I began fantasizing that I had successfully scheduled a cure-all, as though it were a surgery to remove a cancer from my body and, thus, free me of this disease. I felt excited to leave, and it had nothing to do with where I was going. Only the departure mattered.

Sadly, and not surprisingly, within forty-eight hours of arriving at my brother's house in Portland, Oregon, I realized the solution wasn't geographical. In fact, I almost felt worse (if that was even possible). It was as if my body knew the futility of trying to outrun my feelings, yelling at me, "No, no, no, you tricky little weasel. I know what you're up to and that's not how this works. You can't hide from the truth. No, no, no." And then BOOM, the tears came. *Stupid self.*

Upon experiencing this rather quick epiphany, I felt like I had to flee . . . again. That was the only choice, right? I wasn't recovering in Portland, so I had to go somewhere else. I felt as though I couldn't be at ease existing within myself, and I was desperate to seek out an antidote to my sadness and resurfacing depression.

My next move was to head home to Minnesota, where my other brother and his then-fiancée (now wife) were nothing but helpful and

comforting, trying their absolute best to console me when I needed consoling, and to distract me at all other times. "We'll keep you busy!" they said. Which made me feel worse, because how could this not make me feel better? How could I still feel this way when I was surrounded by love, support, and endless breweries? HOW?!

Now, many months and a few runaways later, cut to London, where I've fled for no particular reason. The hardest part about coming here is trying to explain to friends and family why I felt the urge to pick up and leave. "Oh, a couple of friends have been begging me to visit! I've gotta go. It's for them!" Lies. Such lies. It's true that I know people in London (how oddly pretentious does that phrase sound?), but by no means were they begging me to make an appearance. They weren't even asking. I invited myself. It's kind of sad when you think about it—choosing to be that distant from my entire life, and not owning up to it.

Again, I wish to reiterate that running away, for me, had absolutely nothing to do with the destination. It was all a journey of hope that would be deemed successful only if I left but wanted to stay; if I boarded the plane back to the States, sat down in my seat, looked through my camera roll filled with photos, and those memories brought a smile to my face and peace to my brain. Memories that made me miss that place and want to return again one day. If that happened, I told myself, then this runaway would run back to where he belonged with a new glow about him. Rejuvenated. Repaired. Happy to go; happy to return.

London was the first trip that did that for me. There was something about the days that seemed so long that made me giddy to exist in every minute of every hour. I booked a tiny, and let's be honest, shitty hotel room, which had a bed and a shower right next to each other in the same closet-sized space. There was a desk in the corner, with a kettle and all the fixings to make English breakfast tea (which I embraced fully and made on the daily), plus a single sash window that looked out onto the busy streets below. That was all I needed, all I wanted. Every day I would sleep in because, for the first time in a while, I had nothing to wake up for. No reason to get out of bed early. No emails to be answered. It felt like I had not one single responsibility. For the first time in forever, I enjoyed the mundane doings of an average day. That week, my job was to solely exist . . . and I found it liberating.

It fostered an even stronger sense of independence within me, and I felt more detached from our ever-connected world. I was forced to make plans. I was left to my own devices. And I had to sit with my own thoughts and decisions because of the massive amounts of alone time I had accumulated. I'm not saying that running away always works, nor should it be viewed as the solution to our problems when life feels like too much—because it isn't—but on this occasion, for me, London worked wonders.

Here's what I also know: matters of geography don't erase matters of the heart, soul, and mind. No matter your mental state, and no matter the amount of distance you put between you and your problems, leaving rarely solves anything. Problems follow us to locations; they travel with us to all corners of the earth like a permanently attached carry-on. No one can outrun a difficult time or emotion. Not even Usain Bolt.

For a while, I think I labored under the false impression that running away meant I could leave a problem behind and almost forget about its significance. Wrong. That's so wrong. The only way to crack a real problem is to face it. Look your issues dead in the eye and sort out the beef between you.

For the first time in so long, I realized I was okay with just me. I didn't need someone else to be constantly around to make me happy. That was something I had always known deep down but never been forced to understand. In leaving, in putting so much distance between myself and "home," I discovered that I was ready to face my reality and look into the whites of its eyes. Things weren't going to get better magically; they were going to take time and effort. And I had to do this for me. My heart can't mend until I apply the Band-Aids. My mind won't clear until I get rid of the baggage. My self-love and appreciation won't return unless I work toward remembering why I'm great as an individual. My worth is not defined by others; it can only be defined by me.

By no means did I conquer everything on that one London trip. I refuse to sit here and pretend this was a revolutionary moment that brought puppies and rainbows. I'm not going to paint a fantasy just to sound inspirational. But it did lead to an important breakthrough. I still don't know where the ultimate destination is, but for me, life is about finding new paths and connections, and figuring out the twists and turns and ups and downs as you go, encountering all the roadblocks along the way. I'm curious to see where I go with this new mind-set. Only time will tell if I feel the need to run away again. I'm guessing that I will at some point. But who knows? Maybe I'll choose to sit with that urge, keep my feet grounded, look my discomfort dead in the eye, and work it out. Maybe staying put is what the courageous do. Yeah.

I'd like to be brave next time.

that one pink door

i desire
to be the
single pink door
on a street
filled only with
tones painted
unmemorable

london

these streets are full of life
beers clink on the corner
neon gleams in the cobblestone puddles
i leap over
moving toward a destination
i know not of
but there lies the fun
of having no plans
there lies the excitement
of being in my own company
who knows what could happen
who knows where i'll go
or what i'll do
a horn beeps
the stoplight goes green
i'm off
the night engulfs me

daytime

You know those times when you're so utterly relaxed that you genuinely can't think of a single problem in your life? Well, I find myself experiencing that feeling right now, and I want to attempt to capture this rare moment, this best of feelings, in writing. So, here goes:

I'm lying supine on my couch. My feet are up on the armrest and my head is resting on a cushion as the sun streams in, filtering through the leaves of the palm tree silhouetted against my open window. I feel warm but cool at the same time, as if I'm the same temperature as the air in the room, as if we've somehow achieved equilibrium, existing peacefully together, inside of each other, in sync. I watch the swish-swashing palm fronds, softly tickled by the breeze.

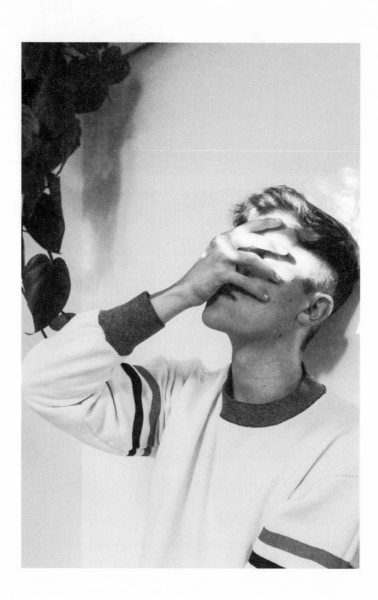

When I close my eyes, I see a pale orange form and feel as though I'm protected from reality, excluded from all expectation, utterly safe in this spot. My eyelids part for a second—the living room appears to be the brightest shade of baby blue. When I close them again, the orange has shifted to the softest shade of lilac. I become aware of my breathing, my quiet exhalations. In my mind, I'm wandering through a field of tall grass, feeling nothing but peace. The day and time escape me. My schedule and plans are nonexistent. I shift my body and curl up, fetal-like. Why can't I feel this worry-free joy all the time? This sense of peace. Such inner calm.

I wish I knew how to induce this state. Instead, it seems to find me from time to time, when it's ready. I'm happily greeted by its warm presence, as if it has shown up to help me through the day. I welcome its soothing effects but also know that it won't stay long; this feeling is fleeting, which is what makes its random appearance so magical.

After enjoying the slow minutes, which feel like long hours, I stretch, open my eyes with the most subtle smile, and return to my day. Thank you, strange state. It's nice to be greeted by your goodness, and I look forward to seeing you again. Until next time . . .

about last night

7:51 a.m.

it rained last night
    i dreamt of you
        and me swimming in
the ocean's waves, softly
      swaying us from side to side

still hurts, not gonna lie

the love, the anger

i saw in those eyes

all of me

Ever since I was a young boy—and I place the blame squarely on my midwestern upbringing for this one—I've been guided toward modesty. Being humble, and thinking of others before myself, was not the right way but the *only* way. Now, that sounds like it would be a good thing, right? WRONG. (Well, maybe not an all-caps wrong, but definitely not fully correct.)

You see, the older I get, the more I understand what it means to walk that fine line between "selfish" and "selfless." In many situations, and contrary to what we've all been taught, it often benefits us to think of ourselves before anyone else.

It's strange to think we're brought up in a world that judges us for putting ourselves first. Somehow, to think of ourselves first and others second has come to sound so incredibly selfish—and that just makes my stomach churn and my teeth grind. How unfair! How misguided! Because here's what I've learned (and what no one seems to teach us in life): you have to make YOU a priority and think in terms of what's good for yourself and your higher interests.

The older you get, the less other people are going to make you a priority. You must speak up for yourself, because everyone else is doing the same. Being selfless shouldn't mean self-sacrificing, in the same way that being selfish shouldn't mean being self-absorbed. There is a middle ground to be explored here.

The people I spend the most time with regularly hear me say things like, "Yeah, whatever you want!" or "No, no, really! I'm okay with anything! YOU choose!" (My friends reading this right now are rolling their eyes because they know it's true and find this trait to be constantly annoying.) But these phrases spill from my lips unconsciously. I can't help it. I don't even think about the options. I simply allow others to make the decision for me—or for them. It's for them, not me, you see. (Look at me thinking they're deciding for me. HA!)

I have forever put the needs and wishes of other people ahead of my own. It's how I'm programmed, and I fear it's how I'll always be. (Okay, how did I manage to make this sound so damn dark so quickly? This is fixable. I. *Am*. Dramatic.)

And yet, 2016 has been the year of discovering me. The other day, after a therapy session, I had a subtle epiphany while sitting in my car, staring out over the steering wheel, gazing into the cloudless, light blue sky. *Me . . . Meeeee. ME. Think about me for a change*, I thought. *Why am I always thinking of him/her/them? This habit needs to stop. This is MY life—precious and unique and worthy of being treated as such.*

I might've started speaking aloud—I tend to do that when I'm having an epiphany. It's actually empowering to verbalize the thought (even though I must have looked like a crazy person yelling to myself from within a locked car, sweating profusely somewhere deep within the Valley. *Ick.*).

During my aforementioned therapy session, I had experienced a powerful realization about how much I relegate my own needs to appease or please others. That's the thing about "Minnesota Nice"—everyone is *sooo* accommodating!

My therapist continually asks, "But Connor, what do YOU think about that?" or, "Connor, how do YOU feel about this?" And somewhere around the fifteenth session and the fifteen hundredth, I started to wonder why I constantly assume how other people are feeling, doing, thinking, or caring. I don't know about their life. I have no control over other people. I have only myself. ME. That's all I know for sure . . . and I barely know that "me" because I've thought about everyone else for so long. *stares up from the large pile of tissues on his lap, looks at therapy lady with jaw to the ground*

Now, back to the scene of me sitting in the hot car.

By the time I had turned the key in the ignition and started to drive home, I had resolved to put *me* first, in thoughts, words, and actions.

With this goal in mind, I had a plan: whenever I dwelled on thoughts of someone else's interests, especially when they were antithetical to my own, I would visualize the word *ME* in its all-caps glory. My mind's eye would focus on the physical form of the word and trace its lines several times over. It's amazing what started to happen once I did this. Eventually, with practice, my mind flipped a switch, and I began to think differently. Granted, lifelong habits can't be undone overnight, which is why I still find myself doing this mental exercise today; I did it in my spin class this morning, in fact. (A friend told me to go, and goddammit, I was going to do it for ME!)

Luckily, this exercise (not the spinning) has proven effective and really helps! Call it a retraining of the mind, undoing old habits and pressing reset. It has also proven to be a healthy reminder that we all have to take care of ourselves first and foremost *before* helping others. Instead of thinking of an action as *selfish*, with all the negative connotations that this word carries, I view it more positively as "looking after myself." More observant readers will have noticed the dedication at the front of this book: *for me*. It's there for a reason: I need to start living for myself, being proud of myself, and cheerleading for myself. Doing things for me. It's a skill I'll refine my entire life, a mindful act that I intend to put into practice every single day.

Obviously, there will be plenty of times when I'll have to put others first. I don't want to be completely self-centered. Common sense will tell me when I need to make another person the priority. I'll always need to compromise in friendships and relationships . . . as long as I'm not compromising myself in the process.

When friends are choosing where to eat, I'm not always going to put up a fight ("I'M LEARNING TO LOVE MYSELF, AND MYSELF WANTS CHEESECAKE FACTORY"). No. That might be a little much. I'll go where they want to go and be happy with it. I'll find something I like on the menu. When a sibling is having a rough day, I'll stop my life for a moment and offer comfort. I can put myself on hold to help someone I care about.

I'm not suggesting for a single second that we stop looking out for one another and being considerate. Being considerate of others is something I will forever hold near and dear to my heart. I'm simply saying there's a healthier balance to be struck.

I've gone through so many life transitions in a short period of time. Adolescent Connor, High School Connor, College Connor, California Connor, Openly Gay Connor, and Present-Day, Whatever-I-Am-Now Connor. And all these versions of me are COMPLETELY different. It astonishes me how much I've changed and grown in just six years. It's terrifying, really. One reason why these versions of myself are so different is because I've slowly learned what it means to become myself, to be true to myself. The connecting factor has come through self-realization.

I've slowly grasped that to be yourself you must know yourself. All the alternate versions of myself have come to fruition because I took the time to find out more about me. As soon as I quit worrying about outside influences and began worrying about what's on the inside, that's when a shift happened. That's when I progressed.

I remain a work in progress and will be to the day I die. Right now, I'm trying my best to simply figure out who I really am. But I'm willing to bet that after this phase, I'll go through another, and another . . . and so on and so forth. But for now, it's all about me. And that's okay.

hook-ups and come-downs

just for tonight

no strings attached

it felt right

it felt wrong

necessary evil

takes its place

no queue but there's a wait

the sun is rising

our eyelids should be falling

so this is what it's like

to be just as the rest

living on night highs

hand in hand

with little rest

slowly but surely

sour and fester

thank you

but i'll pass

too full for seconds

quick, save yourself

before they offer dessert

the dark spot on the back of my otherwise effervescent mind

I won't forget my first year at college. Not because it was especially fun, or filled with endless wild escapades, or even packed with memorable stories. That's not the case. All I remember are the dark clouds following me around, day in, day out, along with the feeling of being boxed in, trapped in an inescapable loop of not being me.

I remember the depression. Or was it a funk? A mere episode? I don't really know for sure what it was. There is no paper trail or second opinion because I kept it to myself. All I knew at the time was that I was nowhere near happy, and that's the most difficult part when those clouds roll in—knowing something is "off" but not understanding what it is exactly, or why it's happening, which, in turn, makes it impossible to explain to anyone else what's wrong. It's a feeling of being trapped in a dark, hazy room with no glowing EXIT sign in sight. The sad thing is that I still find it difficult to understand and express to this day. You can try to articulate the mood and flesh out what it is, but it's never fully accurate. Just know this: I'm not me when I'm depressed. I'm somebody else.

Before I dive in, let me preface this by saying I am not a specialist in mental health, nor am I trying to be. This subject matter is still largely unknown to me, and I'm learning new things about it every day. But what I do know is my own experiences with it. If nothing else, I am an expert in myself, and I would love to teach you what I've come to learn over the past five years of living with this dark spot on the back of my otherwise effervescent mind.

It's all so bizarre. I can't pinpoint the exact day or time during college when depression first took hold of me, but the deadened feeling disturbed me. It was as if the person I saw in the mirror had become unrecognizable, seemingly overnight. *Who am I? How did I get here? Why does nothing interest me anymore? Nothing excite me? Nothing matter?* A rain cloud had suddenly appeared over my head and wouldn't go away. This wasn't sadness. I was not sad. This was something entirely different. This was utter defeat. I felt lower than the floor. And what I now believe to be depression began to affect me. With this newfound awareness, and in addition to the other strong emotions I was feeling, I became deathly scared. Suddenly, my future terrified me more than ever before.

What's more, my grades were slipping. I had no inclination to be social. I was silently crying myself to sleep for no particular reason. Everything appeared bleak and hazy, until it wasn't—and then I'd feel "normal" again and remember what it was like to be me. To be myself. Normal ol' me. But within a day, week, or month, I would spiral back into the deep pits of sorrow, pulled in by a tide that would hit me hard without warning and wash me out into a deep sea, lost in its waters. It had no mercy or consideration.

One of the worst parts was going through this by myself. And the hardest thing is trying to explain the inexplicable to other people, especially when they have no personal experience with it. It couldn't be more foreign to them. This is what it's like trying to explain depression to someone who isn't depressed:

PERSON: You seem so sad.

ME: I'm not sad. It's different than that.

PERSON: How long has this been going on?

ME: I'm not sure.

PERSON: When do you think you'll get over it?

ME: Oh, I wish it were that easy. Right now, it feels like never.

PERSON: Why do you feel this way?

ME: I don't know . . . and that's the worst part.

PERSON: But you're not like this all the time.

ME: It's just there when it wants to be. It goes away and comes back without warning.

PERSON: Can I help?

ME: Just be there for me . . . and don't leave.

It's hard to do this topic justice. It really is. It's scary to talk about because most people avoid it at all costs, whether that's due to the fear of the unknown or simply because they don't want to say something inaccurate or be offensive. What I find is that most people don't under-stand the distinction between depression and sadness, though they're two completely different things. Sadness isn't synonymous with de-pression; depression is so much deeper than sadness. It's hopeless-ness. It's despair. It's not something that you can simply pull yourself out of, like a bad mood that will quickly pass if you distract yourself long enough. Sadness is a mood. Depression is an illness.

The word *depression* is thrown around daily. I hear it in far too many conversations. Sometimes it's said glibly or in a joking manner. It's not a joke, though. According to the American Foundation for Sui-cide Prevention, an estimated 25 million Americans suffer from de-pression, with 50 percent of the estimated 34,000 suicides committed every year associated with this illness. Think about those statistics next time you feel yourself about to say to a friend, "Ugh, I'm like so depressed today." Really think about how powerful that word is, and the history behind it, before using it so lightly.

As a person who has gone under the radar living with depression for years now, many scary questions remain unanswered for me. Will I ever feel fully normal again? Will I ever be "cured" of this? Will it just be gone one day, and I'll never have to worry about it returning ever again? When I'm going through it, I think about these questions constantly.

I will say this: After that first year of college, I somehow got bet-ter. Well, I *felt* better at least. There were no hangovers from tears, or seclusions due to sorrow. I was finally *me* again (or rather, it finally began to feel that way). My second year of school passed by much more easily, without any major breakdowns. I have no answer as to why the depression stayed away for such a long time—I can't attribute it to medication or therapy because, at the time, I didn't try either. To obtain either of them would have meant talking about this deep secret of mine and what I was going through. I wasn't prepared to do that. Of course, I now know that there are amazing support options, to be explored with the help of a professional. There is not an ounce of shame in seeking help. But back then, by some luck of the draw, I got better on my own. And I wasn't going to question it.

Of course, the inevitable happened and eventually I spiraled again.

Six months after moving to California in 2013, depression struck like a giant wave crashing down on every aspect of my life, pulling me into its riptide. At the time, I floundered like before, going under, not understanding the "why." Looking back, I now believe it was triggered by a few things: I wasn't happy with my living situation, I remained in the closet, and my first gay relationship—one that I kept secret—wasn't going the way I had hoped it would. The fact that such an important thing was kept hidden from everyone I cared about was a pressure on its own. But taken together, all of these stressors culminated in many silent breakdowns, which turned into bigger and bigger deals that took their toll on my well-being. The tears were as silent as my state of nothingness.

That's the thing that few understand about depression: It grips you to the point where you don't feel, can't think, and aren't motivated. Sometimes, you feel as though you can't even function. It holds you in abeyance, keeping you hovering over the edge. It doesn't matter if you have a good relationship with family or friends, or if you're rich or poor; depression doesn't respect such things. Depression isn't necessarily a symptom of growing up in a bad home or having a bad childhood. But here's what I've found (and why I'm writing about all this): it helps to talk. Open up. Be brave. Let someone in. Anyone. Or

just let someone sit there and listen to all the irrational thoughts you want to unload at his or her feet.

Being in the future (I'm from the future . . . *woOoOoOoO*), I now know that silence never helps anyone in a crisis. We're all going to face struggles in life—that is an unavoidable side effect of living. It makes us human and is one of the greater truths that connects us as a species. For me, being alone during depression made things worse, but a combination of pride and terror ensured that I kept it private for years. Only recently did I tell myself that it's okay to ask for help. It's completely okay to not take on the world alone, and to have another person share the weight with you.

No one will judge you or view you differently for being vulnerable, because they, too, have once been there themselves in some shape or form. Friends who care will empathize with you. Family who love you will do the same. Only with the assistance of my friends and family did I get to where I am today. They gave me a hand when I was down, and they pulled me back up. It may not have always worked, but they tried; to me, that meant the world. To this day, it means the world. I owe so much to so many and I'm proud to say that.

So instead of going into isolation with your depression and giving it power over your thoughts (that's what fuels it), give voice to what you're feeling. Let someone lend you an ear, and lay it all on your listener. I swear, talking shifts something inside; it provides a release, and it will release you, even if just for a moment. Over time, those moments will accumulate and allow you to assemble into a stronger version of you. A version that will need less and less help and be able to handle things, for the most part, by yourself. Rest assured, it gets easier. It gets better. It remains worth it. The rain clouds will disperse. Keep at it.

a monster in the closet
a beast on the edge
a burden to no one
yet his toes curl the ledge

somebody else

i am not myself these days
i appear to be somebody else
i look in the mirror
i do not see me anymore
i wake up in the morning
i do not feel like me any longer
i am not myself these days
i appear to be somebody else
i want the old me back

the pages i hope you never have to read

You've made it here. I'm sorry about that. I'm so, so sorry. I don't want you to be here. I don't want anything on this page to make sense. Because I wouldn't wish this place or state of mind on my worst enemy. This is one chapter that I don't want you to understand.

Breathe. Slowly, deeply. You'll make it to the other side soon. Trust me.

For anyone who doesn't understand what I'm talking about, that's okay. That's amazing, in fact. It means you don't know what it is to experience the pain of depression, to go through this dark place blindly. Turn to the next section if you like. Skip along. But for those who need this, I'm here. Let's continue. Because I know exactly what you're going through.

Right now, you doubtlessly feel overwhelmed by a flood of bleak, negative thoughts washing over you in a continuous cycle, pulling you into a downward spiral, telling you, *You're worthless. You have no purpose. You're no good. You. Are. Pointless.*

Do not, I repeat, do *not* believe these thoughts. It's not you talking; it's something else. A thought doesn't reflect reality; it dissolves as quickly as it arrives . . . unless you fuel it. So do what I do: withhold that fuel and focus the mind on what you know. You *know* you're a good person. You *know* you have goals, hopes, dreams, and ambitions for a bright future. You *know* you will leave your stamp on this world. You *know* your work is far from done. What you perhaps don't realize is that one day, from much higher ground, you'll look back on this period of your life and laugh at the struggle that you got so needlessly immersed in. You will learn what I'm quickly learning: a positive thought can be planted just as quickly as a negative one arrives, and they both come from the same place—the mind.

Here's a second reminder to breathe.

Now, try visualizing something that brings you happiness, whether it's a person's face, a beautiful destination, a baby, a puppy, a memory from the past, or anything else. Picture it. Concentrate. Remember what it feels like to see/experience/enjoy it. Feel the warmth. Let your insides bubble. Breathe. Wipe away the tears if you have them. Breathe again. And now, if you're up for it, say something positive about yourself. Out loud. Verbalize it. Trust me, I know it sounds stupid and a little eye-roll-worthy, but positive self-talk works. What do you LOVE about yourself? Name one thing. Just one.

I've been here too many times to count, struggling with the downward spiral of negative thoughts. Boy, do I wish I had a friend at my side at these times, helping me get out of this horrible place. So consider this chapter as your friend, and these pages as your voice of reason. Unlike the misleading whispers of false thoughts, these pages do not lie to you. They state the facts. You do have worth. You do have a purpose. You are loved. You are wanted. And should your self-doubt creep up and scoff at you and say, "No, I'm not," know that this is your depression trying to keep you in a negative loop. Don't give it that power. Don't be fooled by your own mind. Counter it with the positive.

You have control over your thoughts; thoughts do not have control over you. They're like little dirt specks on the windshield of life that you simply need to wipe away. There will be more—they will keep coming, sometimes relentlessly—but you will wash those clean as well. You can and you will. We give dark thoughts our power. Why would we ever think that mere thoughts are stronger than us? They're not. We can outwit them. Rule them. Survive them. They represent internal stormy weather . . . and all storms pass. Remember, this state of being will not last forever. Not only the state you're in at this very moment, but the state you've found yourself in for hours, days, or weeks, if not months. You CAN beat this and live the life you know you deserve. You might need to work a little harder than some, but, hey, they need to work harder than you in areas you find easy. We all have our struggles that we must face every day. It's not fair, but if life were fair, then we'd be in utter shit. Can you imagine if everyone got EVERYTHING they wanted? No. NO. I can think of at least six people that the world would not thank for that.

Are you still remembering to breathe? Good. Keep going. It's getting easier, right? You're doing beautifully. Keep the oxygen flowing and the positive thoughts coming. You know that positivity exists—you only have to sift through the rubble a bit.

Never forget, even when you think differently: I love you, and so do so many others. This page is here for you whenever you need a reminder, but so are so many people in your life who care about you. A friend, a sibling, a parent, a teacher, a therapist, a counselor. You have options galore, even if you can't see them clearly in this moment.

You're okay. You will be okay. Breathe deeply one more time.

Now get up and get out into the world. It misses you.

a bitter pulp

i refuse

to let this world

abuse

my already

beaten soul

into a pulp

so bitter

a mouth

would pucker

at its first taste

recoil in fear

from the boy

twisted into a knot

morphed into a newborn

hopeful of his future

with innocence unknown

too precious for a

sunken reality

already set up

to set him down

go on, light up

like a patch of dry brush

burn, baby, burn

brighter than the sun

for eternity

and ever more

if only the universe will permit

conversations with my therapist

FRIEND: So, what else have you got going on today?

ME: I'm gonna finish up some work, throw my laundry in, then head to therapy.

FRIEND: *WHOA!* Wait, are you okay??

ME: Yeah . . . why?

FRIEND: Who hurt you? What did they do to you?!

ME: What? No it's—

FRIEND: TELL ME HIS NAME AND CONSIDER HIM DONE!

ME: No, no, no. It's fine. *I'm* fine. Seriously, you can calm down. Therapy is simply a nice way to talk through anything I'm struggling with up here. *points to brain*

FRIEND: Oh. *pause* Well, that sounds . . . kinda nice.

ME: It is. It's really nice.

FRIEND: Hmmm . . .

ME: *awkward silence, changes topic*

If you ever want to throw a stick in the spokes of a general catch-up conversation with a friend, try telling that person you're in therapy. Nine times out of ten, you'll be met with an incredulous look, a dropped jaw, a furrowed brow signaling your friend's concern that something is gravely wrong—that you are, in some way, disturbed, unhinged, or on the verge of some breakdown. And maybe you are . . . but that's definitely not always the case.

Talking openly about therapy makes a lot of people feel incredibly uncomfortable. I suspect it's because they don't really feel like taking a good, long look at themselves—how they tick or why they behave the way they do. Some people want to avoid feeling too much out of what I presume to be fear that they won't like what comes afterward. Consider me the opposite; I simply want to better myself by understanding why I think, believe, and act the way I do. Besides, going to therapy doesn't mean anything is wrong with me—or you. I repeat for the people in the back of the room: GOING TO THERAPY DOES NOT MEAN ANYTHING IS WRONG WITH YOU. Did that register loud and clear? What it does mean is that you're interested in developing some self-awareness. Therapy turns on every light inside so that we're better equipped to navigate our way through the challenges of life, relationships, and careers.

The problem is that mental health has always had a strange stigma attached to it. But whether you're struggling with depression, anxiety, a loss, a breakup, or heck, even an annoying friend who bugs the shit out of you every other day, it's perfectly normal to seek a professional's guidance. I've been attending therapy sessions off and on for the past two years, and I have nothing but nice things to say about the experience. Well . . . I mean, the act of talking about my problems can actually be horrible, but the process, and what I learn about myself, is worth it. It's like having a friend who will listen without judgment, and then offer up the most empowering insight and wisdom about yourself *to* yourself. Who wouldn't want a dose of that every now and again? I hadn't heard of people regularly attending therapy sessions until I moved to California. In Minnesota, where I grew up, this subject matter remains quite taboo. But, like most things, as soon as I became aware of it, I realized it was no big deal. In fact, I began to see how necessary and healthy it is.

The first time I ever attended a therapy session was just over two years ago. After hearing one of my friends talk so openly and honestly about his therapist, I asked if he would mind giving me her contact information. He agreed, and I sent an email inquiring about a consultation. After a few days, I received an email back saying I could come in the next day! I shuddered. *Oh my gosh . . . this is so soon.* It felt like I was going on a blind date or something. *I don't even know this lady! How am I supposed to tell her the things I don't tell anyone?!* But I knew I needed it, so I sucked up my fear (and several anxious tears) and agreed to meet her.

It was so . . . uncomfortable at first. It really was like going on an awkward first date. I felt like I should ask her questions about herself. But was that inappropriate? *Maybe I should just tell her all about me, and by the time the hour's up, I won't have to talk about anything sad! No, no, that's the whole point of this. UGH.* But eventually we found a natural flow to our conversation. (I attribute it all to her because, frankly, it's her job, she does this all the time.)

I was shocked to see how quickly I became comfortable with this woman in just an hour's time. Before I knew it, the hour was up and I was on my way. I don't remember laying my heart on the table for her, but I do remember utilizing every minute of that session and feeling good as I left her office. And wasn't that the entire purpose of being there, to leave knowing more and feeling better about myself? I think I did just that and called it a job well done. And that continued for more and more sessions to come. It just got easier. Well, not easier; I inevitably opened up about everything and broke down along the way, but that's also the point so, I GUESS IT WORKED.

The conversations I have with my therapist vary drastically, and they largely depend upon what I'm going through at any given time. There have been many periods when I haven't attended a session in weeks (or even months when life just seems to be at its best), which tends to mean I've found some sort of equilibrium. But then I think, *Hmm, I should probably go back to her to make sure I'm doing all right.* That sounds kind of wrong, if I'm being honest. I mean, I should know if I'm fine or not. But what I've learned is that I tend to have several subliminal, stressful forces acting on me on any given day. I keep things bottled up and put myself under a lot of self-imposed pressure, trying to figure everything out on my own, and trying to get by without stabilizers. There are other days when I walk into a session thinking that it will be a wasted hour, and I emerge having talked about a handful of things that I didn't even realize were bothering me. Not only am I a front-facing mess, I'm a deep-rooted one, too. ISN'T THAT JUST WONDERFUL?! But that's what a good therapist does: he or she extracts information, insights, or realizations that you weren't expecting, which in turn make you question yourself beyond what you would normally be comfortable asking. Therapists push you to talk and push you to understand. It's quite magical, really.

Which sounds better: a) I have a lot of stressful things going on but keep them to myself, or b) I have a lot of stressful things going on but I choose to talk about them until I ultimately work through whatever the issue is.

If you chose "b," then DING, DING, DING, you are correct, sir/madam/whatever pronoun you prefer or identify with most.

In my two short years of therapy, I've come to understand that talking about certain struggles actually does help untangle them. It doubtless sounds like a crazy concept to many, because so many people associate therapy with horrible, unfixable things, wrongly believing that any person who needs "a shrink" is "broken" or "messed up." That's not the case at all. Improving our mental health is one of the most important investments we can make. We're happy to spend time toning and shaping our bodies, so why not get our minds in shape, too? You would never shame people for getting a haircut or a massage, or going to the doctor because they have a cold, so why make them feel weird about doing the same for their mind?

I would love to live in a world that does not stigmatize mental illness or shame people for seeking help regarding their mental health. Our minds are the most precious part of ourselves. It's truly where we reside, and maintaining that important piece of ourselves is worth so much. Therapy has helped me more than I can tell you. It's been a friend when I felt like there was no one else. It has shed light at the end of an otherwise dark tunnel. The great part is that there are moments when I need it and moments when I don't. There's a sense of progression when I realize I haven't felt the urge to attend a session in a while. It's almost as if I received the help I needed and no longer require a crutch to hold me up. Even merely typing this reminds me of how light my mind feels today. How easy it is to exist with a healthy head on my shoulders. As long as I can appreciate that, I'm happy.

i don't think people

find themselves

until they're lost

only then does

their journey begin

your

unhappiness

will not bring him back

it will only further

destroy

you

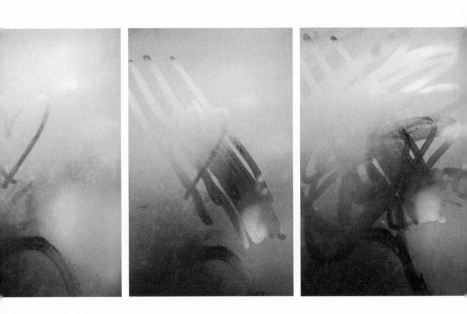

before it happens

mixing, turning

no reason

churning, burning

no reason

i could throw up

as we go up

i begin

a venture

back down

full circle

F our years ago, I attended business and art classes at college, never really believing that business—or even art, for that matter—was for me. I had a good sense of the subject matter but zero passion. None. Nevertheless, I still chose to major in business for two reasons: 1) I heard it was easy, and 2) everyone else told me to. Two of the WORST reasons ever.

I was an idiot, somewhat self-sabotaging my own future by being so blasé and caring so little. I imagined I could coast through, the same way I coasted through classes in high school without feeling overly challenged. Learning came easily for me. What didn't come easily was a sense of direction, or any kind of conviction about what I ultimately wanted to do with my life beyond the next few years.

At school, a vast majority of my peers KNEW exactly what dream career they wanted. Meanwhile, there I was, standing still at the center of a four-way stop, not knowing which way to wander. Once high school came to an end, my classmates soon got into their "dream school" to study their "dream major," but I felt strangely directionless. There was nothing I felt especially good at or passionate about. And this cluelessness usually sounded something like this:

RELATIVE: So what do you want to study at school?

ME: I don't know.

FRIEND: What are you most excited about for next year?

ME: I don't know.

STRANGER: What do you want to do with the rest of your life?

ME: I. DON'T. KNOW.

Now *that* was alarming. But once I chose to be a business major, I felt the pressure ease because at least I had picked something; at least I now had an answer to the "What are you studying in school?" question that adults bombarded me with every single day of my post-adolescent existence. And yet, inevitably, and not long after starting classes, I couldn't hide my disinterest. I had decided on a fluid major, but did I care? Did I genuinely care? No. Not at all. I ended up daydreaming my way through those two years of college. I stuck with it only because so many people around me told me to keep going. Classes drifted by, and by sophomore year my grades were good again, and I kept learning. My butt was in the seat every day, but my mind never checked in. I was, in many ways, going through the motions. Or so I thought.

Fast-forward to the present.

Look at me now: I have somehow managed to make business AND art integral parts of my life. How did this happen? Where did this come from?! I've blown my own mind! Somewhere along the way, I managed to find my direction, and I found it completely by accident. *Oops, there you are, purpose! WHERE HAVE YOU BEEN?? I'VE BEEN WORRIED SICK INTO A NEAR QUARTER-LIFE CRISIS!*

I started talking into a camera, and wouldn't you know it? My current day-to-day existence consists almost exclusively of art and business. I wake up thinking about what I need to do for my businesses. I often can't sleep because there's an artistic idea I need to flesh out and execute. Building my brand and getting creative is my *everything.* I'm applying skills acquired in college to something I'm passionate about. And, boy, has the light been turned on now.

Flash back to my early days at college.

Okay, Connor, I tell myself, I know you're bored out of your mind right now, but just relax! All this business and art stuff is going to make sense one day! TRUST ME.

I roll my eyes at myself. *Yeah. Sure. RIGHT.*

(I really do need to quit having so much inner dialogue with myself. It's becoming a problem.)

Rush back to the present day.

And here I am. It all makes sense now. This is why we need to pay attention. Because life has a funny way of coming full circle. It tends to push us in the direction we need to go, sowing seeds that might not bear fruit until years down the line. We're being introduced to the right people, situations, experiences, and opportunities all the time, whether we realize it or not. We need to soak up those moments and preserve them. As much as my career was a happy accident and felt unplanned, it was, I can see now, the completion of a circle I started to draw when I first went to college, and even years before that, when I really think about it.

None of us knows what the future holds. Indeed, many futures can feel like a massive unfinished puzzle, with all the pieces jumbled up and scattered across the table. What I didn't initially see was how all the pieces I needed were already there, right under my cute little nose. I just didn't know how to form the bigger picture at the time.

Knowing what I know now, there are a few things I would love to tell my younger self: have faith in yourself and what you're doing, keep on trekking, and trust that everything will fall into place. It's okay not to know where you're headed, so long as you keep moving forward. Just pick up the pieces along the way, accrue knowledge, keep learning, and keep going. The worst thing you can do is stop and stagnate. Eventually, you'll reach a place in your life where you'll stop, glance over your shoulder, see the completed circle, and finally understand the reason why your journey took you down a strange path.

colors

reds and blues
remind me of you
greens and browns
like breakfasts downtown
yellows and pinks
on the beach as the sun sinks
whites and grays
in the bed where we lay

footprints in the sand

an ocean of blue

makes thoughts bloom

of a honeydew

evening bliss

couples share a kiss

while ice cream melts

warm scents smelt

drips of sweat drop

hand held in hand

together sharing this day

on yet another

august getaway

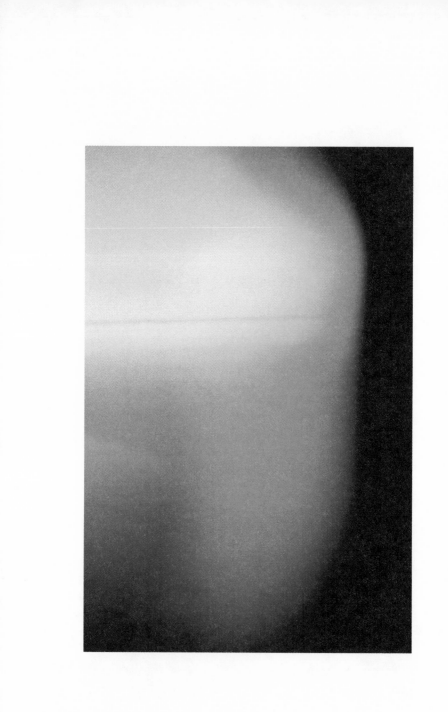

us

rose scents, blanket tents
paper planes, warm rains
soft hair, careless care
another mug, okay one more hug
sunrise kiss, verbal fist
expensive vacation, new destination
midnight flight, flying kites
wait why now, don't leave town
missed calls, social falls
morning tears, solo beers
separate paths, adjacent halves
bend my mind, just be mine
no longer here, my worst fear

wildfire

12:01 p.m.

our love was like a wildfire
it blazed and blazed and took down everything in its path
but eventually every flame must go out

the empty seat beside me

Today I find myself in Portland, Oregon. For those who know me personally (or really know anything about me at all), you know this is my kind of place, full of hipsters and hippies alike, where coffee seemingly pours out of every faucet, runners jog through the night, and a thick blanket of fog often cloaks every inch of the city. At least, that's how I see it.

This foreign yet familiar-seeming land has nearly every single thing that I enjoy in life, and I have no idea why I don't pack up, head north, and just call it home. That's what any normal human would do, right? Ah, but only in my dreams. Or my dream future at the very least.

Recently, I've felt the need to escape the busy, water-less, concrete jungle that is Los Angeles to find refuge in Portland, to quiet my mind and calm my spirit. Okay, I sound like a sort of angelic, all-knowing being. I like Portland and came here to be happier. Because, truth be told, everything is becoming a little too much to deal with. After a mere three years in L.A., the metropolis doesn't seem right for me anymore. Between the people, environment, and lifestyle, it no longer feels like the match made in heaven that I thought it was when I first ventured out west. Oh, and I'm going through a quarter-life crisis due to a horrendous and unexpected breakup that instilled a deep and wretched feeling of loneliness in me, from my toes to my brain, but that's beside the point.

I haven't visited Portland, "the City of Roses," in over a year, and yet I constantly find myself talking about the place, somehow mentioning it in almost every conversation. "What's your favorite city?" people will ask. *Portland*. Easy. No contest. What's more, my brother lives there, which means I have a free hotel and a cat niece and cat nephew to visit, which is a total bonus.

Since arriving, I've spent my days venturing out on my own, mainly because my brother needs to work (like a normal human) and I'd go crazy if left in my free hotel all day long. Honestly, I can't remember the last time I traveled alone and forced myself to be . . . by myself. I've grown to enjoy quiet and alone time, but this is different. This is a forced trip of self-exploration that feels necessary, though I'm not sure why.

I'm willing to bet that a lot of people would hate to do what I'm doing right now; I'm sure many would cringe hard at the mere idea. Because today I am alone. In public. Doing things most people would only do with a friend. *the earth begins to shake, crumbling beneath my feet, and screams of sheer panic break out in a world of utter and absolute chaos*

Yes, you read that correctly. It's CRAZY. *I know*. I should be locked up for even practicing such a *lonesome* activity by my *lonesome*. But I'm experimenting with something I've always been slightly afraid of: hanging out with myself.

I've gotten breakfast, done some work, enjoyed a walk, and even visited a museum. And I called a family member to talk about it only once. Look at me go! This really represents leaps and bounds for someone as introverted as I am. (Well, I'm more of a mix between an introvert and an extrovert, so I guess that would technically make me an ambivert, but that's another chapter for another book for another time.)

Lately, I've had a bit of a forced epiphany. At twenty-four years old, I don't even know who I am when I'm not with other people. I feel almost like half a person, as if part of me has been missing for so long and I'm only just noticing. Even when I'm with close friends, I question who they are, and who I am in their company. And the reason I've been thinking this way, and wanting to spend time alone, is because of recent life changes, i.e., the breakup. It's not *the only* thing, but it is *a* thing. Yes, for the adults reading this, I know this is just a brief phase, and I'm self-sabotaging my social life a bit, but I feel it right now, and I MUST share it with you because I can. That's how this author thing works. Deal with it.

Essentially, I'm finding my feet again as my own person after spending a few years merged with another person. The peril and joy of attachment! Outside of that relationship, I didn't know who I was without my other half by my side. I identified with "us," not "me." I got used to doing things "we" liked doing. Our interests coalesced quickly and naturally as we became one. Also, I didn't seem to notice this merging because it felt so easy, so natural. It's a feeling you won't understand until it's happened to you, but when you find the other half to your heart, it just works. Effortlessly so. It works better than before and you can think of no other way to live than in this beautiful, humming harmony.

Once separated, I struggled to find the line that separates me from him. I frequently thought, *Who am I?* and, *What does this make me now?* I've never experienced this feeling before and I'm going through it as I write these words, so please bear with me. It's new and scary, and I wish with every cell of my being that I didn't have to go through this. But I do, and I am. I half-wonder if I've lost part of my own identity along the way without realizing it, left a piece of me behind and don't know how far away it is. Where did I drop part of myself? Do I turn back and drive along the road until I find it, or keep moving forward and hope it shows up in a different way? That's up to me, I suppose.

When people emerge from a close partnership of any kind— romantic or platonic—and say things like, "I need to find me again," I now totally understand what they mean. It never made any sense before, but . . . I get it now. *Who am I without you? What are we when we're not us? What's my purpose? What do I like? What direction do I want to go in? How do I sleep alone at night? Will anyone go to that weird indie film with me? Who do I text to share the funny thing that a stranger did in public today?*

Am I okay with most of the answers to these vague but very important questions? Hell no. They feel so forced, but maybe they're necessary. Which is why it feels uncomfortable to be hanging out with myself right now. That probably has a lot to do with the void lurking beside me, the memory of another, replaced by the stale air above an empty chair. I mean, when I make an observation about something, who do I share it with? When a question pops into my mind, who do I ask? When I need to know the freaking Wi-Fi password, who do I ask to go find it for me? A stranger?! I would rather drop dead.

Yup, after having the cushioned walls of a relationship's sanctuary ripped away, the feeling of being exposed to one's own loneliness . . . or is it aloneness? . . . is stark. What was once familiar suddenly feels strangely unfamiliar. My own life, and the life I had before him, currently feels unrecognizable. But I don't want to go through life being afraid of my own existence. No. I want my own company to feel like the best company. I want to feel content and peaceful in the presence of myself. I don't want this antsy restlessness. It isn't healthy.

Let's face it: the only person we're guaranteed to have with us on this journey is ourself. Best be happy with that person! For hours on end. Without having to think twice. Without feeling the need to pull someone else into that empty, person-shaped hole beside us.

One thing I've come to learn about myself over the years is that I'm okay being alone for a while, but I don't necessarily enjoy it. Don't get me wrong; I've tried to enjoy it. I really have, but it gets boring after a while. I get why it's important and why I should love it, but I don't. I just don't. Okay, upon further consideration, I actually hate the very idea. It's unsettling to be left with my own thoughts, which grow and multiply and morph into The Worst. My mind, I have discovered, is my own worst enemy, waiting to pounce on me when I'm alone and tear my truth to shreds. Okay, that's a little dramatic, but I do go crazy, dwelling on bleak outcomes and nightmares. Maybe it's my current state; maybe it's my permanent state. I've got time to figure it out. But I am wise enough to know I shouldn't be afraid of solitude. I shouldn't dread the quiet . . . and yet I do.

Transport your attention and imagination back to a coffee shop in Portland that I so swiftly wandered away from.

I'm alone right now, writing away. I've been alone since I woke up this morning. People asked to hang out with me today, but, no, I needed this date with myself and no one else. Just to know I could do it. Just to *remember* I can.

When I first walked into this shop, I was the only person in here, aside from the bizarre-looking, bearded barista with the mismatched shirt/sweater combo. *shudders but also gasps at the fashion* My initial thought was, *Get out of here. What if he's a talker?? He'll TALK to YOU!!* But I stayed and forced myself to ask for the Wi-FI password like an adult. All jokes aside, it actually felt okay to have this moment of solidarity. It's almost as if I'm learning to operate in my singledom, stepping out into a big, scary world all alone. I'm taking baby steps and learning to walk all over again. It's amazing how vulnerable one can feel when going solo, especially after feeling such a part of a partnership.

That's what I'm getting at: when our identity is so wrapped up with that of another, the risk that we all take is losing who we are as an individual within that relationship. And it sucks because it feels so right at the time. We feel so lucky to have that connection everyone always talks about. It's ours now. We've found it. And letting it go doesn't seem like an option.

Often, we merge with someone because we want to dive into that person and relish all that precious time together. But being away from it, I'm quickly learning that in all relationships, we also need to ensure we never lose sight of who we are as individuals—our own interests, our own time, our own friends, and our own sense of self—in the process. You can't lose sight of yourself and only see somebody else. That tunnel vision will blindside you at some point. And so here I stand, guilty as charged for committing that crime. Here I am, in Portland, in a coffee shop, trying to figure it all out again. Forced to find the "me" I lost along the way. While I might be doing a great job at convincing you that I'm okay and figuring it out, I'm not quite there—wherever "there" is—as I write these words. Who knows when I'll get there?

I feel lonely and incomplete right now, but that's to be expected. Or at least, that's what everyone is telling me. "It's going to suck. Really bad. For months and months. BUT then it won't. It will be better in time." I've decided to sit and steep and sulk in my sorrow by choosing to be alone. I need to feel it, not avoid it. The sooner I deal with this, the sooner I can move forward. Disregarding these horrible emotions won't do me any good in the future, so best get it over with now. Rip off the Band-Aid. Go hard. Go quick.

I'm taking this time to tune into myself again, hear my inner voice, determine what I like, and figure out what's best for me all over again. I need to do this. I need to do it for me.

I'll be fine, eventually. I'll get there, whether I'm in Oregon or California or some remote island in the middle of nowhere. This current horror will only help, not hinder. I'll find love again one day. We all do, even though, in our hurt, we vow to never go down that road again. I will not count it out for me. No, sir. When it was good, it was good, and I hold that near and dear to me. Each time we allow ourselves to fall, we learn a little more and grow a little wiser. Yes, I'll find love again . . . and hopefully, next time, I won't lose sight of who I am in the process.

valentine's day

pitch black
air stain
only the sound of my sniffling can be heard in a space
so cold and constricting
messy bed
empty house
i wonder what it's like to not feel this way
will i ever feel better again
i feel as though i'll be alone forever
or maybe that's my interpretation of this silence that
remained nameless for so long

in his arms

it doesn't matter where we are
as long as it's you
and it's me
together
in each other's arms
closer than the eye can see

the other side of the closet

As I sit here typing these words, my eyes glance at my fingers tapping away—and oh, look at my nails, painted a brilliant shade of glittery gold, looking fabulous and leaving me feeling all shades of wonderful. If you could see them with your own eyes, honey, you wouldn't be able to deny it.

Now there's a sentence I couldn't have written two years ago.

I've come a long way in a short amount of time. I've been out of the closet online since mid-2015, and in my personal life since 2014. That blows my mind. I feel like my life has been laced with jet fuel and a hint of acid ever since, propelled into hyperdrive at speeds faster than light. I've changed for the better and feel like a brand-new person, which is something my younger self would never believe; in fact, he would laugh in my face. LAUGH. And not in a subtle, roll-the-eyes, "hehehe" type of way; more like a manic "HAHA! aH hAaaH" don't-be-ridiculous type of way (if you catch my rather informal drift).

It was difficult to envision how much "coming out" would change everything. I had imagined that it would somehow shift everything within me but change nothing externally (if that makes any sense). I didn't want it to alter how people viewed me or interacted with me, but I wanted it to make me a more comfortable, authentic, and joyous version of me—happier in my own skin, truer to my own self than I'd ever been before. If I was completely wrong, then I could reverse into the closet from which I came and hide there FOREVER. Just kidding. Never. I refuse to go back behind that door, among all those hideous teenage clothes. What was I thinking?!

Now, are you ready for me to drop this large cliché bomb? Okay, here goes: once out of the closet, it gets better. BOOM! WHOOSH! Cliché dropped. But really, it's true. The only reason you hear people say that line so frequently is because there's truth in those words (at least for me and those I know). The initial shock of coming out was strange and a bit uncomfortable. But after a few weeks, everything got so much better. The best way to describe it is that I simply felt light, free of a burdensome secret that was weighing on not only my mind but my entire being. After I was able to utter the words "I am gay" to other people, I was overcome with relief, as if saying those words purged built-up toxins from my body. I felt alive again. Healed from the inside. Renewed. Empowered. But allow me to backtrack. I'm sure you want to hear the whole truth and nothing but the truth, right? (I'll assume your inner dialogue responded "right" to that question.)

I want to preface this by saying that, personally, coming out was wonderful. Everyone that mattered to me, together with so many more people far and wide, were nothing short of amazing. I felt supported. I felt safe. I felt downright celebrated. And that's how it should be for anyone who opens up about who he or she really is. Sadly, the opposite is still true for a lot of people in today's world, which is heartbreaking. As much as I would love for everyone to have a similar experience to mine, I know it's important to highlight both sides of the fence. Coming out can be a horrible, traumatic experience, and so, before going forward, please make sure it's safe for you. In an ideal world, everyone's truth would be welcomed and encouraged, but we all know that this isn't the case in many parts of America and the far reaches of the world. I've been empowered by my own experience, and I just want others to feel the same. Moreover, I know the strength and courage it requires. It took twenty-one years to step out as the new me, the real me. But once you do come out openly and live with this true identity for a few months—whatever that may be—it slowly becomes less and less of a thing. The thoughts, doubts, and worries you carried around for so long seem to dissipate. They evaporate into thin air, leaving only the faintest memory behind for the occasional reminiscing.

Initially, it was difficult to feel confident speaking about this secret me. It felt weird to express thoughts that I had long suppressed, such as the times when I'd see an attractive guy walking down the street. It had been so easy for my friends to say, "Okay. Wow. Who's THAT man?" I'd usually nod in agreement but felt uncomfortable going any farther than that. For some odd reason, even though it was no longer a secret to them, I still struggled to be the real me. This whole feeling-like-a-new-human-being thing took some getting used to. So, I began pushing myself to say something, not just think it within my shy self. When I saw someone cute, I started to say aloud to friends, "That man is cute, dammit!!" (But, like, not in an aggressive way because I am a gentleman. *halo floats down from the heavens and onto my head*)

A few months—and a lot of attractive men—later it became easier and easier to find that confident, expressive, true voice. Practice makes perfect—and not only in the things that I verbalized.

For instance, take the first time I attended a gay bar as a single male. Gosh, was that a lot of fun, stress, sweat, and Carly Rae Jepsen! And I mean, *a lot*.

My friends, like normal humans, wanted to go drinking and dancing in West Hollywood, and after a few persuasive texts, they got me to venture out with them. Since going out had never previously been a big part of my life, the night scene felt a little intimidating. For me, it's a vulnerable act to walk into bars knowing that most people are there in hopes they will find someone with whom they'll share the night. I felt that pressure—who knows why—at heavy levels. BUT, I sucked it up and, after getting over the initial shock of being surrounded by so many attractive gays in one tiny room, I let loose and remembered we were all there for the same reason: to have a good-ass time. So, I told myself, *I'm going to have myself a good-ass time!* CAN I GET AN "AMEN"?

You'll be sad to read that I didn't kiss anybody or take anyone home. Not for the lack of wanting to; more because I was having so much fun with myself . . . as strange as that sounds. Remember, I didn't go out a lot, so this initial experience was about taking in the details of the experience and enjoying myself before I moved on to, well, enjoying somebody else.

Much like the new me, going out and feeling comfortable in this new environment took practice. I'm still not what you'd call a seasoned professional on this scene. I still have to try to tip male strippers without giggling and feeling slightly sad, but I'm working on it. OKAY?

You know, I had always wanted to have that experience of a social night out as an openly gay kid/teenager. It did make me wonder what it would have been like had I tried this a few years earlier. Would it have changed me? Would it have made me "me" sooner? I mean, when we were growing up, my straight friends had gotten to meet someone at a bar, dance with a stranger, kiss on the dance floor, the works. Many times (some less legal than others). I was so envious of that. But I knew I couldn't do it because of the whole stuffed-inside-the-closet thing. I grew up feeling almost cheated of such experiences, interactions, and connections. So to now be able to live that opportunity felt like an odd dream. Just to have the option was totally liberating. And terrifying. Gay or straight, the prospect of going up to a stranger in a loud, hectic environment is a scary thrill. But again, practice makes perfect. Learning how to be socially bold is a skill in itself.

What else has changed since letting "the gay" take over?

In a way, I almost feel younger than I am: twenty-four going on sixteen, experiencing everything I was denied years earlier. Crushes make me giggly, going out makes me excited, boys make me nervous, dating feels foreign, and love feels obtainable. *Everything* feels new as the past becomes my present.

When I started experiencing "firsts" that my peers had gone through years ago, it was as though I was making up for lost time, and I simply felt blessed to be given the chance to play this game in which I wasn't able to participate in for so long. That's what coming out represents for me: a second chance. It's like I've been reborn, into a new world with wider horizons and bigger possibilities. It took a long time to get here, but I'm glad I found my way.

I'm lucky I've been given this opportunity because I feel so many people don't get the chance. LGBTQ+ identities aside, people are always hiding who they truly are in some sense. They hold back their most authentic selves for so long, to the point that a "no going back" mind-set is created. It's a total fear of being new and reborn. That's why I feel blessed to have gone through with the decision to be me. What a gift and treasure it is to be true to myself! That's something I could never say and mean before.

Rebirth and reinvention is an opportunity within reach of us all. All it takes is to know who you are and who you ultimately want to be—it doesn't have to be a big show, celebration, or spectacle for everyone else to acknowledge. No. It can be a quiet bloom amongst the other flowers who have learned to show their true colors. All it takes is the drive and desire to seek out the real you . . . and just be. Of course, it's easier to say than do, but if you want it bad enough, there's one thing I can tell you with utmost certainty: it's worth it.

you can't change for somebody and you can't change

somebody for you

new air

let go of the weight
feel yourself float
up into a center
an equilibrium
you so longed for
exhale the toxins
refill your lungs
erase the past
you're here
you've made it
so unsure for so long
so be proud
of the strength
the growth
the change
the depth
you never knew you had
oh my dear
the potential
it gleams on your skin
radiates from you
in a brilliant glow
a sun in itself
so bright
it's hard to look away

an old friend

today

i said it

for the first time

in a while

i felt it

inside my chest

i mean it

deep in my mind

what a strange

thing it is to feel

a feeling you

nearly forgot existed

this vessel

moving through your system

like a boat down a stream

tug, tug, tugging away

an old friend's voice

familiar and calming

it's nice to see you

please do stay awhile

we have some catching up to do

just you

and me

together again

let's hope for longer

than the last time

give you time and you may regret

give me time but i won't forget

don't waste it

Why are we never comfortable with our age?

Kids want to be adults, and adults want to be kids. During our teenage years, we want to stop being treated like children; we want to be taken seriously. And, from what I've observed of older generations, they'd do just about anything to be carefree and young once again, freed of burdensome responsibilities. Maybe that's what we do: wish away our youth, and then pine for it once we understand how challenging adulthood can be. It seems to be a constant battle of wanting what we can't have and not fully appreciating what we do.

Unfortunately, age is something none of us can change. We can try with clothes, with hairstyles, and what we talk about, but none of that can alter the numbers on our birth certificate. So, as much as some of you might yearn to be older, you'll have to wait as long as the rest of us to age. As for those who wish to be younger, well, you might want to stop waiting—that shit ain't happenin'. You're stuck with what you've got; you'd best make the best out of it.

The other day, I was at a business lunch with a woman who was presumably in her thirties. At one point in our conversation, she said, with wide eyes, "How are you such a wise, old soul? Were you always this way?" And in that moment, I either had an epiphany or an early quarter-life crisis (most likely a combination of the two, with an emphasis on the "crisis" part). *WAIT. WHAT?!? ME? OLD? DID SHE JUST USE THE WORD OLD?? Am I comfortable being perceived as a "wise OLD soul"?? When did this happen? I don't want to be old. I'm young and want to stay this way.*

I ended up responding with something along the lines of, "Oh, you know, always . . .," which didn't help ease my newly formed anxiety. I quickly diverted the question to the weather, or the news, or some other bullshit topic. I was over it. I was over *her*. Ah, once again, I was being too dramatic for my own good. And I'm not sure why. I've had the same thing said to me multiple times by different people; never once have I been offended by it. My lunch companion's well-intended words didn't mean to touch a nerve, but they did, and it got me thinking . . .

For as long as I can remember, I wanted to be a grown-up and have more independence and responsibility, to take full ownership of my life. I mean, it is mine, right? In elementary school and beyond, I wasn't the type of kid to ask for help with my homework. I wanted to figure it out for myself. When I landed my first job at the age of thirteen, I didn't accept money from my parents (prior to that, I accepted every penny very willingly . . . thanks, Dad!). I wanted to earn my own living and pay for my own things in order to truly make them, well, mine.

I have since figured out that this is the ultimate goal: to own one's life. I strove to be as self-sufficient as possible, propelling myself toward total independence. That's what everyone must eventually do, so why not get a jump start? I was convinced that better days lay ahead, beyond the tunnel of adolescence, and I was going to drive forward as fast as possible to that destination (while still observing all the driving laws; BUCKLE UP, CHILDREN).

Fast-forward.

I'm now twenty-four years old. I'm here. I have obtained the thing I wanted for so long: the realm of adulthood. The land of taxes, groceries, bills, jury duty, and endless mountains of laundry. But I now find myself looking back and frequently wondering: Have I wasted, and wished away, my youth? Did I waste a period of my life that I'll never get back? That's one scary thought. I got goose bumps just writing that line. But that's a thought I entertain because the idea of being a grown-up issssnnn't quite matched by the sheer reality. It's, um, how do I put this lightly . . . difficult?

Every decision I now make is on me, which is not, for lack of a better word, fun. It sucks. It's hard. It's stressful. It's definitely not all that you think it will be (adults reading this will surely agree). Whether you're twenty-one or fifty-seven, life doesn't get easier the older you get. I'm willing to bet it boils over many times prior to simmering down again. And so my point is this: Don't waste your youth trying to grow up. Because there will come a time when all you'll do is yearn for the kind of naiveté, blissful ignorance, and responsibility-free days that cushion our younger years.

In our youth, we are meant to make mistakes. Like, it's almost our duty to mess up. How satisfying is that? Screw-ups are meant to happen; they teach us about right and wrong and, hopefully, build a constant reminder of "rights" for our futures. We need to fall on our asses—and, if you're like me, more than once (I fell on my ass daily because I'm an uncoordinated idiot)—in our teenage years to better prepare us for adulthood. We endure adolescent difficulties to steel ourselves for the harsh realities of being a human in the world. And the luxury of youth is that most of us don't have to pay for, well, anything: clothes, food, fun, rent, heat, air-conditioning, and those little chip-bag clips. Yup, even *those* cost money. EVERYTHING costs money, and money takes time to earn. SO much time.

You'll realize none of this when you're young, because it's not your job to understand yet. Your job is to go to a building for eight hours a day, fives days a week, and learn about the world and its complexities. How cool is that? I'll take it! I'll have what she's having! Give me YOUR job! Of course, it's only with the benefit of hindsight that I fully appreciate how incredible it is that we each have the opportunity to dedicate our lives, for a time, to school . . . and growing up. It's a privilege that goes underappreciated. I wish I had respected that more at the time, but *c'est la vie,* I suppose.

On paper, yes, I am a legal adult. I live on my own, have a job, pay my bills, do my taxes . . . the works! But the catch is this: I most definitely don't like to consider myself one. I'm no longer a kid, but I still don't feel like an adult . . . and I kind of like that. I feel lucky to have had this realization while caught between two phases of my life.

In fact, I kind of hope to feel this way for a majority of my years. I'm forever young, happily suspended in the middle ground.

When that lady told me I was "old," I really shouldn't have freaked out, because it was a compliment. She saw me as a child but heard me as an equal. That's special . . . and rare. I've managed to chameleon my way through different social circles and adapt to whatever my surroundings are. Maybe one day I'll fully move on to adulthood and be content with that transition. Until then, I'm happy to enjoy the ride as the grandpa-child that I am, happily living each day at the age I am.

innocence in february

never been
before
what will i be
after
all that matters is
during

i want it now

I'm going to make a prediction: the bane of this generation's existence will be its instant and constant access to everything . . . and let me tell you why in two simple minutes.

We have become "the NOW generation," to (unintentionally) borrow a phrase from a Black Eyed Peas song. We want things fast, and we want them now. No delay. No lag time. We're so conditioned to our fast-lane living that we think it's normal to have everything we need or desire available to us at the click of a button, at any hour. Food, electronics, a ride, directions, an errand, research, laundry, hook-ups, sex, drugs, alcohol, you name it. Anything. No need to wait. No need to develop patience. You want it? Then have it! It's easy!

It seems like a total and utter miracle to have the world at the actual tips of our fingers, and it is! But at what cost? While the advancement of technology is an amazing thing, and it helps make our lives more convenient in many ways, I worry that this constantly connected, always-online, dependent-on-apps reality is going to turn us into a lazy, entitled, almost diva-like generation. Everything is about having our needs met for our personal and immediate gain. We're talking warp speed here, folks. Otherwise, three stars! But instead of snapping our fingers, we can now click a button on a screen we carry everywhere with us.

Nothing exemplifies this want-it-now expectation more than the world of dating. The online world of dating, to be exact. One swipe, based on appearances alone, puts you within one step of a hook-up . . . if, that is, your swipe gets "a match." Feeling lonely? Swipe! See who also wants company. Feeling horny? Turn on your location setting and see who is equally stimulated in your neighborhood. Looking for love? Go online—scores of people projecting the same romantic dream are available RIGHT NOW! Act NOW. (Can you tell I'm a little cynical with this whole dating-app business? Maybe *traditional* is a better word than *cynical*, but you get me.)

That's not to say I'm against this need for immediacy. I think I'm just frightened by how omnipresent it's becoming. I don't want to lose my sense of human connection, and it feels like that's happening at a rapid rate.

Gone are the more organic days of two people locking eyes across the bar, or bumping into each other in the street and striking up a conversation in which sparks seem to literally fly from their eyes. Okay, such chance meetings may not be dead yet; they can still happen (my romantic soul insists that they can!). But the general trend appears to be shifting toward virtual connections, and I can't help but wonder if this is happening because we're all so . . . lazy?

Why make the effort when we can speed-date our way around our phones, exchanging text messages rather than exploring the chemistry of a verbal or physical interaction? It takes a while for me to understand the way my closest friends text, let alone a pure stranger. How am I supposed to know what you mean by "hah"? Are you actually laughing or is that a dry, sardonic "hah"? HELP.

I'm not even sure that this immediate access to potential mates has any meaning, or serves our best interests. We now live in an era where we pick and choose on looks alone and hook-ups are completely normal. It has become weird to have less than a handful of sexual partners. I'm not slut-shaming you if you do; if you want to sleep around, by all means, go for it! It's just starting to feel like it's the only option at this point, and I like options! For me, there is no connection in mindless hook-ups conducted without feeling, emotion, or true intimacy. I thrive on conversations, stories, and personality. Without any of that first, it's hard for me to want more. We are in danger of becoming vain, empty shells looking for something to make us feel . . . what? Connected again?

And the saddest part of this boom-time in dating apps, or any app, to be frank, is that it spills over into our attitudes and how we treat other people and services. It's an attitude of, "If you don't want what I need NOW, or have what I desire THIS SECOND, I can find it elsewhere. It's simple: I don't need you. If you don't have anything to offer, why are you still here?"

Does that sound harsh? Feel too cold and mechanical? Well, maybe I'm merely reflecting what modern-day "dating" has become. Certainly, it's what I'm detecting from the friends and subscribers in my world. And it scares me.

How ironic that in an ever-connected technological world that's all about advancement, we're becoming less connected as people, too wrapped up in our never-offline lives, putting us at risk of dehumanizing ourselves in our hunger for the quick fix and the must-have. I can't even put my phone down anymore. It's like an itch that needs to be scratched every few minutes or I'll go insane. Whether it's to check an app or answer an email, it all adds up because my phone is never turned off. I'm always available, compulsively peering at pixels.

And then, even when we're with other people, how many of us are on our phones? (Which is basically like adding more people to the group.) Our devices are becoming the walls we build between each other. They're the walls we first encounter when getting to know one another and they're the walls when we're a couple, removing us from the present moment that we're meant to enjoy.

Okay, I'm guessing that some of you might be frustrated or strongly disagree with me, standing here on my pedestal. That's okay. This rant could simply be due to the time in my life in which I'm writing this, or the fact that I just binge-watched *Mr. Robot* and feel like going on a near-psychotic rant. I'm just venting, so please don't come after me here. I come in peace!

It could also be due to daily observation, and the fact that I'm seeing countless people get "lost" in this instant-access world while viewing it as the new norm. And those mere observations are all I have. I don't have answers or solutions. I don't know where any of these social trends are leading, but I do hope that we can stay aware and remember not to lose sight of one another in the rush to have whatever it is that we want. Even if it is convenient, that doesn't make it right. Just be aware and be careful not to get lost out there.

listen to this

what's better
than empty bonds and
meaningless connections
well, that's easy
everything

the

only

thing

        fair

about

this

life

is

how

unfair

it

is

my

    eyes

        lie

            on

                your

                    lying

                        eyes

you are who you want to be

You can convince yourself of literally anything, no matter what anyone tells you. But I don't think any of us put this to use in a positive way often enough.

Here's what I mean: If you think you're ugly, you'll be ugly. If you think you're stupid, you'll be stupid, and so on and so forth. The more you personally reinforce the negative things you think about yourself, the more of a reality they become, and the more truth they appear to have. But the good news is that it works both ways. On the flip side, if you think you're confident, you're fucking confident. If you think you're fun, you'll be the life and soul of the party. It's all about self-perception.

I've noticed this seesaw of negative-positive in myself, and I've tried to put it into practice. Have I always been confident or bold enough to try and be the funny one? My god, no. Not at all. It wasn't until a few years ago that I began surrounding myself with people who radiated certain qualities I admired; only then did I learn that I could have what they did . . . if I really wanted to. Growing up, I never saw myself as super-attractive. I never believed my jokes were the best, or my intelligence was as high as my peers'. It's not as if I didn't think I had those qualities, but I came to the false belief that others did things better than I did. I'm not sure what flipped that switch, but once it was turned on, I had the powerful realization that I could do anything and be anyone I wanted to be.

In recent years, I have come to understand the benefit of giving myself internal pep talks. When meeting up with friends, I know that wearing something amazing will make me feel confident. When I put on dope clothing, it's almost like I'm wearing a costume and become a whole new person. Right before leaving my house, I'll look in the mirror and know that I have nothing to worry about in the looks department if I simply enjoy my outfit.

Confidence is something we can all wear. Take it from me, it can be learned and acquired over time. Confident people were not born confident. Like any skill, they were taught *how to be.* So, if others are to see me as confident, then I need to believe it, too. It's almost like acting. A sort of "fake it until you make it" notion. And that's what I've been doing in so many realms of my life.

Can't dance? Well, try your best and look like you're having a blast so that people don't even care, or notice, if you're hitting the right beats. Bored with a conversation that leaves you feeling sidelined? Try bringing up a recent news topic, documentary, or political issue. If you thrive on discussions that engage you, you will come across as intellectual, regardless of whether you believe you are or not.

Granted, all the above may seem daunting, but change takes time. None of us can transform our personalities overnight. But, eventually, we reach a point where we no longer feel like we're faking it. The more we work on a trait that we wish to develop, the stronger it gets, like a muscle. The more we believe something about ourselves, the more we reprogram our thinking. The more we dwell on the positive, the less the negative can touch us.

None of us are stuck with the hand we are dealt. We can shuffle the deck and deal the cards out again. No one can tell you who you should be. You need to be the person you want to be. You are, quite simply, who you want to be. Think it. Own it. Be it.

And you can. For you.

repeat this until you believe it

it will be worth it
please don't forget
don't let him change you
don't let them hurt you
don't let you convince you
that it won't be
because it will

the five-year plan

People always seem to want to know about your future while overlooking your present. One question I'm frequently asked is, "Well, where do you think you'll be in five years?" Hell, even if I thought about it really hard, I couldn't tell you what I want to do *one* year from now. In fact, I don't even know what I'm having for dinner, let alone what I'll be doing in the year 2022.

For me, this is by far the most bullshit inquiry you could ever make of the younger generations. Between the ages of sixteen and twenty-six are arguably some of the most important years of a person's life. That's when we're bombarded with experience after experience, and when change hits us from every direction like a slap in the face.

From the perspective of my nineteen-year-old self,

my current reality is the last thing I would've imagined, but here I sit, living it. The years when we transition from adolescence to adulthood should be entitled "Expect the Unexpected" . . . and all our ideals, hopes, plans, and expectations should be treated with caution. Even now, at the ripe old age of twenty-four (yes, I just compared myself to fruit), I've come to accept the fact that I am in the heat of transformation.

Anything is possible at this age. ANYTHING. So why, oh why, would I even begin to try to fathom what my existence will look like in five years? Why would I limit all possibilities and all unknowns by trapping the future into some kind of framework, tainting my potential? My reality cannot conform to people's fantasies, or their need to know what the future holds.

You'll notice that the older generation—the generation that seeks stability and security and doesn't like us not having firm, rigid plans— are more prone to asking this question. On multiple occasions, it has come across as incredibly condescending to me, in a very "Oh, what will you do when your fake little Internet hobby falls through?" type of way. When people are bold enough to ask me, I can't help but roll my eyes and flip the question toward them. "Where do YOU think you'll be in five years? Please take your time; I can wait."

Ultimately, they laugh because, like me and everyone else, they have no fucking clue. And that's okay. They want to respond with the same answer I do: "I'm not sure." Age might relieve many things, but it doesn't ease our discomfort with uncertainty. The mind seeks clarity, but our souls prefer to wander into ambiguity. It's OKAY to not know your future. It's acceptable to have no idea what you want to do. Don't let anyone trick you into thinking otherwise.

An offer, opportunity, breakthrough, or brain wave could happen at any moment and change the trajectory of your life. Surely the key to life is being open to such a possibility.

Five-year plan? That's hilarious. The more I type those words, the more I laugh. Chuckle? Giggle? Giggle. Ah, yup, there it is.

Here's what I think (and it constitutes an answer of sorts): in five years, I hope I'm successful, happy, and healthy. Heck, I hope for the same in fifty years. I wouldn't mind if I'm a multimillionaire living in a giant seaside mansion with a hot supermodel boyfriend, or in a modest townhouse with a nine-to-five husband and kids. It doesn't matter. If the "successful," "happy," and "healthy" boxes are checked, I'm okay with whatever I'm doing and wherever I am in the world.

Let none of us be fooled into thinking we need to know what the future holds. Everyone's been brainwashed into thinking they know or *should* know. We'll be all right if we simply keep moving forward. At least, that's what I keep telling myself. So next time someone asks about your five-year plan, maybe shrug your shoulders and admit, "I don't know—I'm happy to see where life takes me."

build and rebuild

born a construction

but made for rebuilding

every move

twist, turn

undoes and remakes

on the back of your nation

along the crest of your brow

placed in details where you lay

imbued with the power to change

you reclaim yourself

at your daily discretion

malleable to the maximum

coiled in a fragile cycle

broken in due time

patiently waiting in the background

born to be you

however false

born to become you

however true

love is selfish and i am greedy

LOVE IS RIGHT
NO MATTER
HOW MANY TIMES
IT WRONGS YOU

kisses

warmth slowly
takes me
like a raft
in a river
rushing through
my internal grid
mind, like
a hive
body, like
a pool
fix my buzz
flip that switch

weekend

take in
the weekend
white sheets
bare feet
movies and warm drinks
walks with arms linked
sundays smell of honey haze
yet taste of lemon sour
funny how bittersweet
things can turn in just an hour after
takeout

when i see the light

lights appear below

there they are

there they go

beams of hope

freedom from the dark

a rush of adrenaline

takes my being

from a city so alive

i see it breathing

i begin to share its energy

the wheels hit the ground

and just like that

i'm somewhere i've never been

i can smell the island air

i'm here

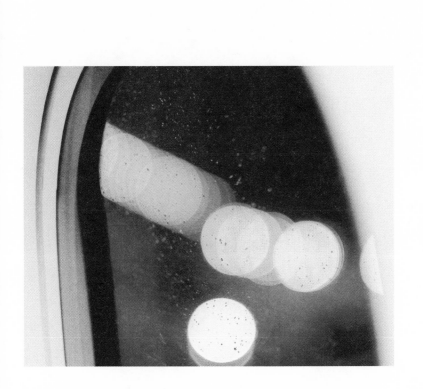

be in touch with reality but always allow yourself

to fall into fantasy

avoiding a cliché has proven difficult here

Renowned psychotherapist Carl Jung once said, "The privilege of a lifetime is to become who you truly are." Think about that for a second: imagine being the unfiltered, no-pretend, don't-care-what-others-think, authentic version of you. Imagine that.

Ask yourself: What am I? Who am I? What makes me *me*? If you had to describe yourself in three words, what would those three words be? Come on now, participate! Don't just read this. Stop and genuinely think about it. I'm waiting! Allow yourself to dig deep and not feel silly about it. I'm asking YOU who you think YOU really are, and what YOU know about yourself. It should be easy, right?

We usually find the answers in our own company, or

in the company of our closest, dearest friends. We see our true selves in moments when we're not trying so hard to impress and be liked. So psychoanalyze yourself to your heart's content: Are you smart? Thoughtful? Strong? Playful? Fun to be around? The sweetest of souls? Socially awkward . . . or supremely confident? Made of stern stuff . . . or sensitive and easily hurt? Do you need attention . . . or prefer it when others do all the talking? Are you a go-getter . . . or a plodder? Calm . . . or anxious most of the time? (This is the kind of stuff they ask early on in school but never seem to follow up on.)

Okay. So what three words would I use to describe myself? I'll join in, too. *Hm, hm. hmmmm . . .*

Driven. Visionary. And oh-so-giggly.

That's a weird combination, but accurate. See, it wasn't so hard! (Although you don't know how long it took me to place the words on this page, and you never will. Hahahaha.)

Now, you, too, should have your three words . . . so forget them. Put them aside and try to see yourself from another person's perspective. How do friends regard you? How do you think strangers see you? How do your nearest and dearest best describe you? (Are you a little afraid of this? I am!!!) Often, the reflection of ourselves is best seen in the "mirror" that a friend, relative, or stranger holds up.

Lately, I've been thinking a lot about self-perception and how much of it is actually a reality versus a fantasy, a self-delusion. We all have a belief about who we are; there is always the story we tell ourselves. But HOW do any of us truly know the answer? I fear that most people, if asked, would just tell us what we want to hear; it would all be nice and complimentary, but probably not honest. People tend to be too polite, even when asked to be otherwise. It's the same reason I never know if I should tell the person I'm talking to that he has food in his teeth. *Hmm.* Maybe that's not exactly applicable here, but you know what I mean. Politeness often blocks honesty. That seems to be the way of the world. Nobody wants to be the one who tells a person some uncomfortable, perhaps unflattering, home truths. You'd be pretty twisted to enjoy being that kind of messenger! (And now I can't help but think that someone, somewhere, is reading this and thinking *Muhuhahahah . . . I LOVE DOING THAT!* If that's you, put down this book, you sicko! I don't want you touching any of these aesthetically pleasing pages with your evil sausage fingers.)

Okay. Baaaaack to reality. I'm trying to be serious here . . .

This is an interesting topic to me, because at what age do we figure ourselves out? Twenty? Thirty? Fifty? EVER?? There's no one answer. Like everything in life, some of us will wake up faster than others. Some people figure it all. out in their mid-twenties; others might make it to old age before self-awareness kicks in. We all know that one person who seems to know EVERYTHING, and has somehow managed to find a cheat sheet to this reality. I hate that human. (I want to *beeeeeee* him!) I wish there was a formal age or set time when all of life's secrets are uncovered, and that we all live more consciously and happily ever after!

Personally, I'm chasing that privilege that Carl Jung referred to: a true understanding of myself. I'm learning more about who I am on a daily basis. It's a constant search, but I'm lured by the promise of the discovery of gold nuggets, especially as I face some of life's most difficult questions, moments, and situations. It's a bit like using a magnifying glass when looking for that earring you dropped on the floor—everything looks like a blur; there is no clarity. But the harder you look and the longer you search, the clearer things seem to become until BOOM—it just appears in front of your face in crystal-clear 4K HDR (I bought a TV recently and that's the only reason I know wtf that means). Who we are, what makes us tick, and what's in our highest and best interests comes into sharp focus . . . if we're willing to look inward. When I compare myself to who I used to be five years ago, I see different people with different interests, goals, ambitions, and even personality traits. I've grown—and there's nothing more satisfying than that feeling. I've slowly turned into the person I'm meant to be, and I can only imagine that I'll continue to grow and change and evolve for years to come, which is exciting! If I've gotten this much better in five years, how much more will I enjoy myself in ten years? That's the hope for me, for you, and for everyone else: that one day, someday soon, we will look in the mirror and confidently see the reflection of our truest selves, the person we know we are and were always capable of becoming. But most of all, the person we are happy with and proud to be.

to my dearest future

Hello, wherever and whenever you are. I'm not quite sure when you'll be reading this, but I'll assume it won't be for at least five years. No no, let's make it ten, minimum. Yeah, that should allow enough time to go by, and for life to look very differently from how it does now. I don't have a crystal ball in my *immediate* possession, but I suspect this future will involve a new place, maybe a new job and fresh ambitions; a pet, perhaps, as well as a potential husband and kids—you know, the works! At the very least, time will bring change, to the extent that I probably won't even recognize myself. My stomach is in my throat just thinking about it (in a good way, I swear).

Now, without sounding too melodramatic or self-indulgent here (famous last words), I'm writing this in the year 2017—and you're currently killing it. You're living in Los Angeles and acting as your own boss for not one, not two, but THREE companies. Last night, as you doubtlessly remember, you delivered a seven-minute speech to a room packed with people; it was the night you were honored as the Game Changer of the Year by GLSEN, an LGBTQ+ charity. Julia Roberts, Kate Hudson, and Jim Parsons were there! You're writing your second book (obviously), and your clothing designs are currently being distributed by Urban Outfitters, an international company worth over one billion dollars. INSANITY.

Of course, all this will seem like ancient history to you, Future Me. Treasured memories from days gone by. Yet you have to recall how unbearably overwhelming it all felt, right?? Even while typing this chapter, I'm low-key annoyed at myself for admitting that. It's cool. It's SO fucking cool and needs to be appreciated as such! Are you raising your eyebrows at me for being so giddy? Are you looking back and thinking, "Awwwh, he has no clue what's about to happen" (for better or for worse)? Damn, I wish I could know where you are. I wish I could know what you're doing and where life has led you. This all feels like I'm putting a message from my current self in a bottle and throwing it out into the ocean, unsure when, where, or even IF my future self will receive it.

Anyway, I digress. Let's continue to look ahead.

In my previous letter to my Past Me, I was able to connect the dots and offer reassurances. With this letter, I can't even see the dots, let alone the joined-up lines. But here's what I do know, and I'm pretty sure it'll resonate: forget all the things that don't matter (possessions, wealth, fame) and focus instead on what you or someone else is going through. Because what they're going through, and how they emerge from that experience, tells you exactly who they are. That's what

makes them *them*. That's what 2016 was for you: a building year. Sur-
viving your first traumatic heartbreak, which meant dealing with the
loss of a best friend and a subtle identity crisis, was, by no means, an
easy thing to cope with, but I'm sure it makes a lot more sense to you
now. It only takes time, they say . . . whoever THEY are. After all, you
now have the luxury of hindsight that I can't possibly have. I'm sure
you have other loves to measure it by, too. Heck, you're probably looking back on this time with a wry, knowing smile. Laughing at these
pages (in a modest way, as you do when you're uncomfortable). I bet
the idea of being almost emotionally paralyzed over such a young love
feels as ludicrous to you as Donald Trump being the 45th President of
the United States of America. (We survive this, right? Please tell me
Kanye doesn't become our 46th President . . . please.)

Yeah, you'll remember 2016 for being an intense year, full of madness
in work and in your mind. Filled with new emotions and experiences
colliding together. I'm sure the lessons, in love and in life, have continued
to come thick and fast, and hopefully you continued to learn from each
one. Only you will know how many more bruising relationships—and
elections, to be frank—I still have to face. I don't even dare hazard a guess
as to how many times you've loved and been hurt again. But as strange as
it might sound, I actually hope that you've experienced it all over again. In
suffering, you've found a greater understanding and appreciation for all of
life's wonders. You're still trying to believe it every day. One morning you
convince yourself it will all be worth it, the next you're down and believe
it all to be worthless. Pain is love and love is pain. It's all oddly necessary—and nothing is permanent. I want that teacher in my life. I'm sure
you have more scars on your heart by now. I'm sure your edges have been
rounded, and you grasp more firmly what this world is about.

On the flip side, I hope you've encountered, in these ten-plus years, love in all of its forms. Do you have new friends? Are you in contact with your old ones? (Don't make me remind you to reach out to them. You know you love hearing from your swim team car pool, your college buddies, and your Los Angeles friends alike. Shoot them a dm, or if social media is dead, just give them a call!) Friends aside, I hope you feel the love you give to them in return. You're such a sap, filled from your toes to your nose with adoration and empathy; your feelings are oozing out of your soul. That's one of your greatest qualities, and I know, deep down, all you want is to receive that from another person. I know you will find it—if you haven't already.

Another hope, and an odd one at that, from Present Me to you, is that you *don't* have complete harmony in your life. Strange request, I know. I hear people around me day in and day out wishing for peace and quiet, yearning for a certain level of simplicity that I don't think can ever be obtained. (I mean, I hear myself wish for it every other day, too, but I don't ACTUALLY want it . . .you know?) I don't think that's how things work. Not for you, anyway. It doesn't get easier for those of us with desires that can never be satisfied—not from greed but from passion. You better not have eased up on your ambition; that inner fire should be cherished and utilized because that's one of your favorite aspects of your personality. I hope it's burning as fiercely as ever. I never want you to lose that hunger for more. More information, more feelings, more experiences, more peaks, more valleys, more connection, more disconnection, more, more, more. I find so much purpose by seeking a deeper understanding of all the ins and outs of life, and I never want to lose that. That's what I've learned to love about myself: that inexplicable desire that's rooted in who-knows-what.

I hope you're stronger, bolder, and more self-confident. Right now, as I write this, you're so insecure in ways that you can hardly verbalize—and you rarely do. You're getting so much better at getting out of your bubble and your own head, and you're taking vast strides toward self-improvement. You'll remember these days—the days you conveyed a quiet but calculated confidence to the world—but most things are calculated nowadays, which sucks. Maybe you're no longer so aware of your actions, body language, hairstyle, the words coming out of your mouth, and everything in between your ankles and brain. Maybe your mind is no longer a hive filled with buzzing bees. Maybe you can rest better and feel more comfortable in yourself. I do hope you can appreciate how hard I tried to be. . . better at being me. I hope you give me credit, too, for slowly learning that I am who I am, and I should not become an alternative, false version of myself. I think it'll take time to accept that the real me is good enough.

Does this letter feel like you're reading an old journal entry? Are you wishing that you could write another letter to your past self? Woah, very meta. *Wow, writing this makes me feel a strange type of crazy. Okay, back in I go.*

Ultimately, I hope you're happy. Yet another important cliché, but that's my biggest wish for you out there in the future. I can't wait to see and feel how *you* feel about me right now, to appreciate the exhilaration, the love, the dizzy highs, the head-in-the-clouds naivety of being twenty-two, twenty-three, twenty-four. If only we could talk or text. (Someone make an app for that, STAT.)

I will say, your career is forever confusing to you and the world. As amazing as it sounds to be able to do everything, it would be nice to pick one thing and pursue it fully. I'm sure that's what you're doing in the future. I hope you're more focused and moving in a single direction.

As long as it's creative, I don't give a fuck what it is. Fulfill me with the greatest you have to offer, and satisfy my cravings. If I know me, I'll always find a way to make my own way. Rarely do I fail because I usually believe I can do anything. It took a while to truly believe that, but even in the present day, I know it to be true. Take a moment to remind yourself of that if you've forgotten it in the future. You can do anything.

I hope you better understand that others can add to your well-being but they can't create it. You, and the happiness you cultivate within, are all you have, from beginning to end. Everything else is a chapter of an unknown length. But I want those chapters to be rich, full of color, adventure, and life. Each is important, and all are rooted in you. When I catch up to you, and stand where you stand now, I want to feel the joy and look back at me—at us—with pride and satisfaction, devoid of regrets. As I write these words, aware of the blank pages that lie ahead, I know and trust that everything will be fine; that we'll be fine. Everything is always fine in the end, if you will it to be. I'm not naive enough to ignore the inevitability that things will go south again at some point. That's life. It's shitty, but it's consistently inconsistent. I refuse to live in fear of slipping on banana peels and falling into pits—sometimes, it's for our own good. Each experience will shape me into a damn good human being. And I have a feeling you're a damn good human being.

If you continue to be a good person, then that's wonderful—that's really all I can hope for. So keep striving for your goals, marching forward, and pursuing your passions. That's where your happiness lies. I'm right behind you, headed your way. I look forward to hearing all about the journey, sharing laughter, and looking back on the memories with fondness. One day. Until then . . .

notes to them

Ah, yes, this is the time when I get to thank all the wonderful people who helped make this book possible, in some way. Here's a list filled to the brim with love and adoration:

To my editors, Steve and Jhanteigh: Thank you for sticking with me all the long way from book one through book two. From the stressful midnight texts to the encouraging midday calls, you two make my author life an honest pleasure. You've become the greatest of friends along the way and I'm grateful to have found you.

To Judith, Ariele, Jackie, Albert, Dana, and everyone else at Keywords: This project only saw the light of day because of each and every one of you. Your hard work, care, and stunning ambition means the world to me, and I am beyond appreciative to have worked with this team, not once, but twice.

To Sam and Cory: Thank you both for your work on the visuals, inside and out of this book. They, specifically, were held near and dear to my heart and wouldn't look half as pretty without your touch and input.

To my agent/friend/part-time therapist, Andrew: We've been friends and working together for nearly four years now and, although very close at times, have somehow managed not to strangle each other. I attribute so much of my success to the endless hours you put into me and my career and am oh-so-grateful to have you in my life. You're a total boss and I love you.

To my attorney, Ryan; my book agent, Cait; and my publicists, Chelsea and Doni: From the contracts to the projects to the interviews that follow, you are all simply wonderful at what you do and I couldn't be happier to have you on my team.

To my family, Mom, Dad, Dustin, Nicola, and Brandon: Thank you for being, for the most part, the only consistent aspects of my life. I can count on all of you for absolutely anything at any time, and that is beyond comforting. You keep me centered, remind me to be good, cheer me up, and make me laugh. Not a day goes by that I do not appreciate all of you for that. I'm a lucky one. Love you with all my heart.

And finally, to you, the readers: You are as deeply important as all the others. You make what I do possible and give a seasoning of meaning to all the work I put out in this world. Thank you for not only reading the book but taking in its words and searching for your own meaning amongst these pages. That brings indescribable happiness to me—along with the lengthy list of other things you do to support me on a daily basis. I am beyond grateful to have been gifted with that support. I appreciate all that you do for me and would not be where I am without you. So, thank you.

about the author

Connor Franta is an award-winning internet personality, *New York Times* bestselling author, dedicated LGBTQ+ philanthropist, and entrepreneur with millions of followers across his social media platforms. His first work of nonfiction, *A Work in Progress*, was a *New York Times* bestseller and the Goodreads Choice Award Winner for Best Memoir & Autobiography (2015). He is the founder of the lifestyle brand, Common Culture, which offers superior clothing, premium coffee, and a variety of undiscovered musical talent under Heard Well, the first label powered by social tastemakers. To learn more, visit ConnorFranta Books.com and @ConnorFranta on YouTube, Instagram, and Twitter.